GROUP ACTIVITIES FOR COUNSELORS

Sally Elliott

Cover design: Nancy Clark
Editor: Dianne Schilling
Illustrations: Dianne Schilling

Copyright © 2015 (Revised Edition), INNERCHOICE PUBLISHING • All rights reserved

ISBN - 10: 1-56499-091-5

ISBN - 13: 978-1-56499-091-4

Student experience sheets may be reproduced in quantities sufficient for distribution to students in counseling groups utilizing *Group Activities for Counselors*. All other reproduction for any purpose whatsoever is explicitly prohibited without written permission. Requests for permission may be directed to INNERCHOICE PUBLISHING.

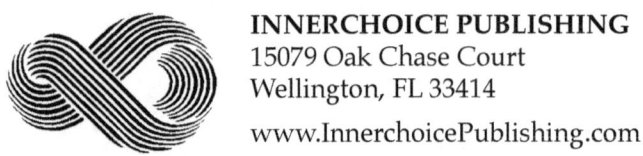

INNERCHOICE PUBLISHING
15079 Oak Chase Court
Wellington, FL 33414
www.InnerchoicePublishing.com

Contents

Introduction

An Introduction to the Activities 1

Starting a Group Counseling Program 5

Leading Group Sessions 6

An Overview of Sharing Circles 8

Activities

Ice Breakers 15

Self-Concept 31

Communication 51

Peer Relationships 71

Conflict Management 93

Succeeding in School 113

Changing Family Groups 135

Cultural/Racial Issues 155

Social/Sexual Harassment 171

NOTE: Some activities in this book involve potentially sensitive issues and therefore may not be suitable for all students. Please review each activity carefully prior to use, making whatever modifications are necessary for the age, maturity, and culture of your students, the policies of your school, and the conventions of your community.

Group Counseling
An Introduction to the Activities

Use and Applications

Think of *Group Activities for Counselors* as a recipe book — a collection of varied recipes for excellent dishes that you can prepare using the skills you already possess and incorporate in menus which you develop.

The recipes, of course, are activities — nearly one-hundred of them. In addition to a number of "Icebreakers," which can be used to warm up any group, the activities are organized into topic areas that correspond to eight prevalent developmental and special-concern counseling groups:

- Self-Concept
- Communication
- Peer Relationships
- Conflict Management
- Succeeding in School
- Changing Family Groups
- Cultural/Racial Issues
- Social/Sexual Harassment

With few exceptions, each activity within a topic area is independent and capable of standing alone. Collectively, the activities should *not* be construed as a developmental program in that counseling area. They are collections of activities to use within the programs that *you* develop. Remember, you are the chef.

School-based group counseling may be therapeutic, but it is not therapy. Most groups are task-related, instructional, developmental, or related to special student concerns. Therefore, before you launch any group, you should have a plan — better yet, a detailed lesson plan. Choose activities from this book that fit within that plan — that have compatible objectives, add interest and enjoyment, and provide the type of structure you are looking for. Simplify activities for younger students. Challenge older students with discussion questions that demand deeper levels of self-examination and higher-order thinking skills.

Basic Assumptions

The activities in this book reflect the influences of an eclectic constellation of leaders and theorists in psychology and education (Carl Rogers, Abraham Maslow, Sam Keen, Harvey Jackins, Thomas Gordon, Albert Ellis, William Glasser, Robert Carkhuff) and several core assumptions about the nature of human beings.

- Every individual is inherently worthwhile and has the right to be self-determining. Furthermore everyone needs and deserves attention, acceptance, and affection, and virtually all behavior is an effort to achieve one or more of these three goals.
- People are capable of solving their own problems. They are resourceful and growth-oriented, and in a healthy, nourishing social environment will flourish.
- Human beings are whole people — not collections of parts. Feelings, thoughts, and behaviors are interactive, relating to one another in a multitude of ways, and all three areas of functioning must be included in efforts to achieve self-understanding and growth.
- In order for young people to be ready to lead fulfilling, productive adult lives, they first need to experience the fullness of themselves. They need to know who they are, how they function, and how they relate to others. They also need to believe in themselves.
- For better or for worse, every intervention that a counselor makes impacts the self-esteem of affected students. Likewise every activity in which students participate either strengthens or weakens their sense of worth and worthiness. Self-esteem is fluid, and constantly subject to change. Changes in self-esteem occur in response to specific experiences — both deliberate and natural — and, in a narrower sense, simply because self-perceptions vary from environment to environment.
- We have charge over our self-esteem and possess the capacity to change it. There is no ceiling on self-esteem. However, the current state of our self-esteem determines the quality of our experience in every situation.
- Successes in life nourish the growth of self-esteem. Self-esteem is neither amorphous nor elusive; it is as tangible an educational target as intelligence, and is enhanced by the development and acknowledgment of personal attributes and identifiable life skills.
- It is the role of the counselor to provide experiences that facilitate the development of these skills and attributes, and to be alert to and acknowledge every increment of growth.

School counselors are well-trained, well-intentioned, highly motivated individuals. You are one of those individuals. Your experience and expertise will guide you in selecting activities from this book and using them as springboards to generate productive group interaction, thereby achieving your educational and counseling goals.

The Sharing Circle.

In each section of this book, you will find at least three activities subtitled "A Sharing Circle." Since each of your counseling group meetings is a "session," and since you will probably be seated in a "circle," the distinction between a group session and a Sharing Circle needs some initial clarification. (The Sharing Circle is dealt with in depth starting on page 7.)

A Sharing Circle is a group within a group. It is a special process that differs significantly from the varied and ever-changing interaction of the group as a whole.

If you've never led a Sharing Circle, be sure to read the appropriate parts of the introduction carefully. Get the distinctions straight yourself so that you can help your students distinguish between the way the counseling group functions and the rules and procedures that apply to the Sharing Circle.

Other Strategies

Group Activities for Counselors utilizes a wide variety of guidance and instructional techniques. The Sharing Circle is a central strategy, but there are others. This section describes several major strategies and presents basic points to keep in mind as you implement them.

Dyads

When first initiated, dyads are probably most effective if the students are allowed to select their own partners. After the students know each other better, ask them to pair up with someone they've never worked with before. If the students tend to shun the opposite sex, announce that you would like to see boys and girls pair up.

Ask the students to sit close to and facing their partner, and position themselves as far away from other students as possible so they can hear their partner. If the number of students is uneven, be a partner to the remaining student.

In most dyad activities, partners take turns speaking and listening in response to one or more topics. Dyads allow maximum self-expression in a relatively short time period and are the most effective way for students to discuss some topics.

Triads

Some triad activities are simply very small discussion groups. Others are like dyads in that the students take turns speaking and listening in response to specific topics. The difference is that the third person in the triad acts as an observer while the other two interact. The observer role is played by each member of the triad on a rotating basis. The function of the observer is to note the behavior of the interacting pair and provide feedback.

Small Group Discussions

Depending on the size of your counseling group, you may need to create smaller groups for portions of some activities. Recorders will need to be chosen in some instances. Occasionally, you may wish to have small groups observe Sharing Circle rules, not because you want to transform the task into a Sharing Circle, but to provide structure and safety. One of the main advantages of small groups is that they give the students an opportunity to collaborate—which facilitates problem-solving and stimulates creativity.

Group Discussions

Almost all activities include a culminating discussion, and some activities are almost entirely discussion. When leading a discussion use your best facilitation skills, keeping these guidelines in mind:

- Questions should be relevant, timely, and open-ended.
- There are no right or wrong answers.
- Keep the discussion focused.

Without being rigid, ask students who introduce peripheral issues to bring them up again when the main discussion is over or at some other time. Digressions can ruin the effectiveness of a discussion, but very often the other thoughts that students introduce are worth discussing, too.

Brainstorming

Brainstorming is a very valuable way to promote individual creativity and group cohesiveness simultaneously. Perhaps the most important thing to remember about brainstorming is that the generation of ideas and the evaluation of ideas are two separate processes. Thanks to this distinction, individuals may contribute their ideas spontaneously without fear of criticism. Brainstorming includes the following basic steps:

- The task or problem is defined.
- The students describe all the ideas they can think of, without evaluating any of them.
- The ideas are recorded.
- The brainstorming is ended.
- Then and only then, the ideas are evaluated.
- A choice or decision is made.

Art

The major objective of art activities is to allow students to express their feelings and ideas creatively. You don't have to be an art teacher to involve students in activities that encourage artistic expression. For example, cartooning may be an acceptable substitute for writing.

Dramatizations and Role-Playing

Besides being very dynamic, acting experiences promote direct, experiential learning. Dramatizations usually involve planning, rehearsing, and performing, and often call for a student director. Role-playing is more spontaneous, and unfolds in a situation that simulates reality. Although the participants are playing the parts of other people, they usually end up playing themselves, as their own values surface.

Role-playing is frequently used as a problem-solving technique in which alternative actions are tested and evaluated. Opportunities for role-playing may evolve from personal anecdotes, real problems, and fictional scenarios. The book also utilizes role playing to promote the internalization of various skills. Behavioral rehearsal is the key to producing lasting change. The ideas listed below represent variations in the standard approach to role-play.

Solution Role Plays. Describe the typical situation to the group. Choose volunteers to play the roles and have them act out the scenario. Interrupt them, however, before the characters resolve their problem. Then form small teams and ask each team to define the problem, brainstorm possible solutions, and choose the solution they feel is the best. Have each team role play its version of the problem and solution for the rest of the group.

The Freeze Technique. Examine individual behaviors within a dramatization by stopping the action at key points in order to point out how the situation may be altered by an attitude, a small action, a failure to listen, and so on. After you stop the action by saying, "freeze," ask the characters why they're behaving the way they are. Ask specific questions such as, "What did (Hector) say or do that you are reacting to?"

Role Reversal.. Changing roles helps students explore both sides of a situation. After the students finish role-playing the situation, have them switch roles and repeat the dramatization. Afterward, ask the students what they learned from experiencing the other person's point of view. Ask them to compare their respective approaches to resolving the problem. Which solution seemed preferable? Why?

Alter Ego. This technique helps students look at possible feelings and motives underlying the actions of various characters in a role play. Station a student, or "alter ego," next to each of the characters in the scenario. After a character speaks, allow his or her alter ego to add comments that express what the character is actually thinking and/or feeling.

Starting a Group Counseling Program

If you have never before managed a group counseling program, the following suggestions should prove helpful.

Planning

Before beginning a group counseling program, it's a good idea to assess the needs of the students, either informally, through discussions with teachers, administrators, and other counselors, or formally through written surveys and reviews of statistical and anecdotal data that might provide clues as to the concerns and issues faced by students at your school.

Counseling groups typically meet on a weekly basis for 6 to 12 weeks, in sessions that last from 30 to 60 minutes, depending on the age of the students.

Don't try to lead too many different types of groups concurrently. Develop a plan that allows you to alternate the kinds of groups you lead, and then schedule those groups several months in advance. Once you begin to advertise, your groups are likely to fill up fast. Having a long range plan allows you to tell students approximately when the next group will begin, rather than simply placing their names on a waiting list.

Gaining Faculty, Administrative and Parental Support

If you conduct a needs assessment, your interest in starting a group counseling program will readily become apparent. If you consider yourself — and are viewed by others — as part of the educational team, you know how to articulate goals that appeal to both teachers and administrators.

Teachers are interested in the academic progress of students, and in alleviating conditions that interfere with that progress — stress, anxiety, behavior problems, preoccupation with family concerns — and will welcome the support that your program offers them. Administrators have similar concerns, and must also deal with parental, attendance, public relations, and fiscal issues. The efficiency of group counseling (providing direct services to several students at once) appeals to administrators.

Most parents want their children to have access to as many services as a school provides. Advertise your groups as an integral, ongoing part of the school program. Let parents know that counseling groups are not therapy groups, but rather are small, interactive learning environments where kids develop important life skills.

Recruiting Students

Once everything else is in place, recruitment should be fairly easy. Here are some ideas:

• Develop a referral form for teachers and administrators to complete when they want to recommend a student.

• Promote the entire group counseling program by publishing a comprehensive calendar of group sessions. Occasionally place the calendar in teachers' boxes, post it on bulletin boards throughout the school, and keep a stack in the office.

• Promote individual groups with flyers and posters.

• Have your plan in place when you visit classes or advisory groups early in the year to explain the school's counseling program. Include a pitch for upcoming groups at that time.

• Keep a sign-up sheet outside your office for students who want to refer themselves.

• Send a letter or flyer home to parents inviting their referrals. Give a brief presentation at your school's parent organization and stay afterwards to talk individually with interested parents.

Screening Students

It's a good idea to meet one-to-one with students who have signed up or been referred for a group. Ask them about their own goals and expectations in participating, and tell them yours. Make sure they are committed to attend, to participate, and to honor the confidentiality of the group.

Use the information gained from these interviews to form potentially productive combinations of students and to weed out students who are likely to disrupt or retard the progress of the group.

Leadership and Group Dynamics

Leading groups is an art, in which natural talent may blossom, but skills can also be developed. It is certainly not necessary to be a professional counselor or therapist to lead wonderful groups. In fact, community volunteers who are willing to dedicate time and energy to facilitate groups often become superb leaders.

There are, however, some qualities and skills that tend to enhance the dynamic of a group, and that facilitators might profit by developing. Among the most important is an ability to listen emphatically, with focused attention, giving eye contact and exercising the blessing of having two ears and only one mouth. While listening, watch for nonverbal communication such as facial expressions and body language. Listen with your intuition as well as your mind. That "gut level understanding" is often very insightful. Validate the group members so they know you heard and understood. This can be done both verbally and non verbally, and provides a sense of trust and comfort. It is also important to know how to help a speaker clarify thoughts, and to invite reflection.

While your primary goal in group

facilitation may be to support the members, remember to take care of yourself, too. Set and keep healthy boundaries. Notice your own body language. It often provides a clue as to "What's happening now with me?" and offers an opportunity to help you develop a comfort level with conflict, intensity and silence. Accept some anxiety. It is normal. As you are real, authentic, genuine and honest, you will be able to acknowledge mistakes and successes. Offer love, respect and trust, even to yourself.

Remain impersonal, rather than personal, compassionate rather than sympathetic. The difference is about staying clear and of service, rather that trying to fix, and ending up taking it home with you.

Listen to the words you select and how you deliver them, especially by monitoring your tone of voice. This sets the stage for encouraging non judgmental feedback and responses from member to member. Also it is important to respond (responsibility), rather than react. Some helpful responses to model might be:

Tell me more …	Sounds like …
It seems to me …	I get the feeling or impression that …
I hear you saying …	I wonder …
I'm wondering if …	As I hear it, you …

Perhaps these qualities and skills seem like a large bill to fill, and truly they are. It may help to keep in mind the potential of the group to positively affect the lives of others. It also helps to remember that you are there to support, not fix. Trust that the answers are inside of each group member. Your job is to nurture their self-discovery and self- healing, rather than to take control and attempt to change or fix.

It might be helpful to think of yourself as a guide who encourages new ways of thinking, feeling and behaving. Create a positive environment by providing structure, setting norms, establishing rules and confidentiality, eliciting accountability, creating safety, fostering learning and expression, supporting sharing, encouraging risk-taking, and promoting healing. All of this promotes positive self-esteem, which supports the members in applying what they learn to life situations. It may sound difficult, but believe it or not, you have already been developing these skills, which you use in forming relationships throughout life. Take inventory, and honor the vast experience you bring to the group. Let this knowledge be your safety net, then trust your heart.

Leading Group Sessions

Initial Session.

The first time you meet with students, clarify the goals of the group, establish some ground rules (e.g., voluntary participation, attentive listening, no put-downs, and confidentiality), and do a warm-up activity that allows you and the students to learn each other's names, become acquainted, and start building rapport and trust.

How a Group Develops

Inclusion, cohesion, and interdependence in a group are not realized without some initial awkwardness, testing, jockeying for position, and perhaps a conflict or two.

Theories of group dynamics point to four stages in the development of a task group. For purposes of school counseling groups, think in terms of three stages:

1. **warming up** — organizing, resolving conflicts, building trust
2. **working** — sharing, gaining insights, accomplishing goals
3. **winding down** — terminating, saying goodbye

Keep these stages in mind when selecting activities and developing a lesson plan. Choose relatively light, involving activities for the first few sessions — activities that promote interaction and build trust. Introduce more challenging activities around the midpoint of the group, when productivity is likely to peak. In the last couple of sessions, consider using activities that help the students internalize and refine the skills and knowledge gained by participating in the group. Role playing and Sharing Circles are excellent choices.

Sharing Circles work well at all stages, but are particularly appropriate when concentrated at either end of a group's life cycle. The circle rules promote sharing and safety simultaneously, which builds trust and helps students become acquainted and comfortable with one another When a group is winding down, the topic-driven nature of the Sharing Circle allows you to facilitate closure by having the student's speak to topics (you can develop them yourself) that promote summarizing, evaluating, integrating, and applying the information and skills covered in the group. For example:

The Most Helpful Thing About This Group Has Been...

A Way I've Grown by Participating in the Group

Something I Would Like to Say to the Group

One Way I Plan to Use What I've Learned in the Group

Something I've Learned in the Group That Will Help Me in School

What I Think Good Communication Is

My Friendship Goal Is

One Thing I've Learned About Change

How I Plan to Promote Better Group Relations at School

What Assertiveness Means to Me Now

Leadership Skills

Even though you have a lesson plan and a curriculum, keep in mind that the students learn as much or more from each other during group sessions as they do from any activity or information you present. An activity is merely a vehicle for interaction. An activity provides the structure, the students themselves provide the substance, and you hold the baton.

As individuals are added to a group, the number of possible interactions between and among members multiplies exponentially. Your job is to orchestrate all of this.

Many of the skills you routinely practice during individual counseling sessions are equally applicable to group counseling — attending, accepting, active listening, and reflecting. Now, in addition, you will need to:

- set the tone
- observe carefully
- model the behaviors you seek to develop in students
- keep the group on task

- connect personally with every member and facilitate connections between members
- involve everyone
- summarize

How all of this looks blended together depends largely on your style. Relax, be yourself, model genuineness, and enjoy yourself in the group.

Terminating a Group

When a group goes well, members are often reluctant to see the last session arrive. All the more reason to imbue the final session with as much purpose and structure as previous sessions, then bring it to positive closure. Here are some suggestions:

- Celebrate the group's accomplishments.
- Recognize students by giving each one a certificate honoring his or her participation in the group.
- Reaffirm commitments to pursue personal goals established within the group. Do it ceremoniously.
- Lead an activity that allows members to connect with each other one last time in a positive way.
- Finish with a group hug.

An Overview of Sharing Circles

The Sharing Circle is a unique small-group discussion process in which participants (including the leader) share their feelings, experiences, and insights in response to specific, assigned topics. Sharing Circles are loosely structured, and participants are expected to adhere to rules that promote the goals of the circle while assuring cooperation, effective communication, trust, and confidentiality. To take full advantage of this process there are a some things you need to be aware of.

First, the topic elaborations provided under the heading, "Introduce the Topic," are guides for you to follow when presenting the topic to your students. They are excellent models, but they need not be read verbatim. The idea is to focus the attention of students on the specific topic to be discussed. In your elaboration, try to use language and examples that are appropriate to the age, ability, and culture of your students.

Second, we strongly urge you to respect the integrity of the sharing and discussion phases of the circle. These two phases are procedurally and qualitatively different, yet of equal importance in promoting awareness, insight, and higher-order thinking in students. After you have led several circles, you will appreciate the advantages of maintaining this unique relationship.

When used regularly, the *process* of the Sharing Circle coupled with its *content* (specific discussion topics) provides students with frequent opportunities to become more aware of their strengths, abilities, and positive qualities. In the Sharing Circle, students are listened to when they express their feelings and ideas, and they learn to listen to each other. The Sharing Circle format provides a framework in which genuine attention and acceptance can be given and received on a consistent basis.

As a counseling tool, the purpose of the Sharing Circle is to promote growth and development in students of all ages and abilities. Targeted growth areas include communication, self-awareness, personal mastery, and interpersonal skills. As students follow the rules and relate to each other verbally during the Sharing Circle, they are practicing oral communication and learning to listen. Through insights developed while pondering and discussing the various topics, students are offered the opportunity to grow in awareness and to feel more masterful—more in control of their feelings, thoughts, and behaviors. Through the positive experience of give and take, they learn more about effective modes of social interaction. The Sharing Circle provides practice in the use of basic communication skills while relevant life issues are being discussed and valuable concepts learned.

The Value of Listening

As counselors, we know that merely listening to students talk can be immensely facilitating to their personal development. We do not need to diagnose, probe, or problem solve to help students focus attention on their own needs and use the information and insights in their own minds to arrive at their own conclusions. Because being listened to gives students confidence in their ability to positively affect their own lives, listening is certainly the helping method with the greatest long-term payoff.

When a student is dealing with a problem, or when her emotional state clearly indicates that something is bothering her, active listening is irreplaceable as a means of helping. Active listening puts us in the student's shoes while she does the walking. It communicates two messages: understanding and acceptance. It is based upon our knowing that the student is the only one who can solve her own problems. She has the most data about what is at issue and, if she can draw a solution from the data, she will have grown a step toward responsible adulthood.

Solutions do not generally come through a single big insight. Finding THE answer is not what usually happens on the path of personal development. A solution to a problem may be as simple as gaining a new perspective. Problem solving is a process that we must learn to do for ourselves our whole life long.

The Sharing Circle provides the opportunity for students to talk while others actively listen. By being given this opportunity on a regular basis, students gain important life skills and self-knowledge. Once they see that we do not intend to change them and that they may speak freely without the threat of being "wrong," students find it easier to examine themselves and begin to see areas where they can make positive change in their lives. Just through the consistent process of sharing in a safe environment, students develop the ability to clarify their thoughts. They are encouraged to go deeper, find their own direction, and express and face strong feelings that may at other times be hidden obstacles to their growth. The important point is that students really can solve their own problems, develop self-awareness, and learn skills that assist them in becoming responsible members of society *if they are listened to effectively.*

Just as the Sharing Circle provides a process for students to learn about themselves through self-expression and exploration, it also teaches students how to be good listeners. The rules of the Sharing Circle (listening to the person who is speaking, without probing, put-downs, or gossip), and the periodic review, demand that each student give active attention to the speaker. Through the regular practice of good listening skills and the positive modeling of active listening by the counselor, the students begin to internalize good listening habits.

How to Set Up Sharing Circles

Group Size and Composition. Sharing Circles are a time for focusing on individual contributions in an unhurried fashion. For this reason, each Sharing Circle group needs to be kept relatively small—eight to twelve usually works best. Young people are capable of extensive verbalization, and you will want to encourage this, not stifle them because of time constraints.

The specialized group-counseling context not withstanding, each Sharing Circle group should be as heterogeneous as possible with respect to sex, ability, and racial/ethnic background. Sometimes there will be a group in which all the students are particularly reticent to speak. If possible, bring in an expressive student or two who will get things going. Sometimes it is necessary for practical reasons to change the membership of a group. Once established, however, it is advisable to keep a group as stable as possible.

Length and Location of Sharing Circles. Most Sharing Circles last approximately 20 to 30 minutes. At first students tend to be reluctant to express themselves fully because they do not yet know that the circle is a safe place. Consequently your first sessions may not last more than 10 to 15 minutes. Generally speaking, students become comfortable and motivated to speak with continued experience.

In a counseling-group setting, Sharing Circles may be conducted at any time during the group session. Starting Sharing Circles at the beginning of the meeting allows additional time in case students become deeply involved in the topic. If you start circles late in the meeting, make sure the students are aware of their responsibility to be concise.

In all settings, Sharing Circles may be carried out wherever there is room for students to sit in a circle and experience few or no distractions. Some leaders conduct sessions outdoors, with students seated in a secluded, grassy area. When conducted indoors, chairs provide the most popular seating solution, however, students may like to sit on the floor, especially if it is carpeted and they can sit comfortably.

How to Lead a Sharing Circle

This section is a thorough guide for conducting Sharing Circles. It covers major points to keep in mind and answers questions which will arise as you begin using the program. Please remember that these guidelines are presented to assist you, not to restrict you. Follow them, and trust your own leadership style at the same time.

The Sharing Circle is a structured communication process that provides students a safe place for learning about life and developing important aspects of social-emotional learning.

First, we'll provide a brief overview of the process of leading a Sharing Circle and then we'll cover each step in more detail.

A Sharing Circle begins when a group of students and the adult leader sit down together in a circle so that each person is able to see the others easily. The leader of the Sharing Circle briefly greets and welcomes each individual, conveying a feeling of enthusiasm blended with seriousness.

When everyone appears comfortable, the leader takes a few moments to review the Sharing Circle Rules. These rules inform the students of the positive behaviors required of them and guarantees the emotional safety and security, and equality of each member.

After the students understand and agree to follow the rules, the leader announces the topic for the session. A brief elaboration of the topic follows in which the leader provides examples and possibly mentions the topics relationship to prior topics or to other things the students are involved in. Then the leader re-states the topic and allows a little silence during which circle members may review and ponder their own related memories and mentally prepare their verbal response to the topic. (The topics and elaborations are provided in this curriculum.)

Next, the leader invites the circle participants to voluntarily share their responses to the topic, one at a time. No one is forced to share, but everyone is given an opportunity to share while all the other circle members listen attentively. The circle participants tell the group about themselves, their personal experiences, thoughts, feelings, hopes and dreams as they relate to the topic. Most of the circle time is devoted to this sharing phase because of its central importance.

During this time, the leader assumes a dual role—that of leader and participant. The leader makes sure that everyone who wishes to speak is given the opportunity while simultaneously enforcing the rules as necessary. The leader also takes a turn to speak if he or she wishes.

After everyone who wants to share has done so, the leader introduces the next phase of the Sharing Circle by asking several discussion questions. This phase represents a transition to the intellectual mode and allows participants to reflect on and express learnings gained from the sharing phase and encourages participants to combine cognitive abilities and emotional experiencing. It's in this phase that participants are able to crystallize learnings and to understand the relevance of the discussion to their daily lives. (Discussion questions for each topic are provided in this curriculum.)

When the students have finished discussing their responses to the questions and the session has reached a natural closure, the leader ends the session. The leader thanks the students for being part of the Sharing Circle and states that it is over.

What follows is a more detailed look at the process of leading a Sharing Circle.

Steps for Leading a Sharing Circle

1. Welcome Sharing Circle members
2. Review the Sharing Circle rules *
3. Introduce the topic
4. Sharing by circle members
5. Ask discussion questions
6. Close the circle

*optional after the first few sessions

1. Welcome Sharing Circle members

As you sit down with the students in a Sharing Circle group, remember that you are not teaching a lesson. You are facilitating a group of people. Establish a positive atmosphere. In a relaxed manner, address each student by name, using eye contact and conveying warmth. An attitude of seriousness blended with enthusiasm will let the students know that this Sharing Circle group is an important learning experience—an activity that can be interesting and meaningful.

2. Review the Sharing Circle rules

At the beginning of the first Sharing Circle, and at appropriate intervals thereafter, go over the rules for the circle. They are:

> **Sharing Circle Rules**
> - Everyone gets a turn to share, including the leader.
> - You can skip your turn if you wish.
> - Listen to the person who is sharing.
> - There are no interruptions, probing, put-downs, or gossip.
> - Share the time equally.

From this point on, demonstrate to the students that you expect them to remember and abide by the ground rules. Convey that you think well of them and know they are fully capable of responsible behavior. Let them know that by coming to the Sharing Circle they are making a commitment to listen and show acceptance and respect for the other students and you. It is helpful to write the rules on chart paper and keep them on display for the benefit of each Sharing Circle.

3. Introduce the topic

State the topic, and then in your own words, elaborate and provide examples as each lesson in this book suggests. The introduction or elaboration of the topic is designed to get students focused and thinking about how they will respond to the topic. By providing more than just the mere statement of the topic, the elaboration gives students a few moments to expand their thinking and to make a personal connection to the topic at hand. Add clarifying statements of your own that will help the students understand the topic. Answer questions about the topic, and emphasize that there are no "right" responses. Finally, restate the topic, opening the session to responses (theirs and yours). Sometimes taking your turn first helps the students understand the aim of the topic. The introductions, as written in this book, are provided to give you some general ideas for opening the Sharing Circle. It's important that you adjust and modify the introduction and elaboration to suit the ages, abilities, levels, cultural/ethnic backgrounds and interests of your students.

4. Sharing by circle members

The most important point to remember is this: The purpose of these Sharing Circles is to give students an opportunity to express themselves and be accepted for the experiences, thoughts, and feelings they share. Avoid taking the action away from the students. They are the stars!

5. Ask discussion questions

Responding to discussion questions is the cognitive portion of the process. During this phase, the leader asks thought-provoking questions to stimulate free discussion and higher-level thinking. Each Sharing Circle lesson in this book concludes with several discussion questions. At times, you may want to formulate questions that are more appropriate to the level of understanding in your students—or to what was actually shared in the circle. If you wish to make connections between the topic and your content area, ask questions that will accomplish that objective and allow the answering of the discussion questions to extend longer. We have left a space on each page for you to note significant other questions that you create and find effective.

6. Close the circle

The ideal time to end a Sharing Circle is when the discussion question phase reaches natural closure. Sincerely thank everyone for being part of the circle. Don't thank specific students for speaking, as doing so might convey the impression that speaking is more appreciated than mere listening. Then close the group by saying, "This Sharing Circle is over," or "OK, that ends our circle."

Reviewing what is shared
(An optional step)

Besides modeling effective listening (the very best way to teach it) and positively reinforcing students for attentive listening, a review can be used to deliberately improve listening skills in circle members. If you choose to conduct a review, introduce it after the sharing phase and before you ask the discussion questions.

Reviewing is a time for reflective listening, when circle members feed back what they heard each other say during the sharing phase of the circle. Besides encouraging effective listening, reviewing provides Sharing Circle members with additional recognition. It validates their experience and conveys the idea, "you are important," a message we can all profit from hearing often.

To review, a circle member simply addresses someone who shared, and briefly paraphrases what the person said ("John, I heard you say...."). Be sure that everyone who shared gets a review.

The first few times you conduct reviews, stress the importance of checking with the speaker to see if the review accurately summarized the main things that were shared. If the speaker says, "No," allow him or her to make corrections. Stress too, the importance of speaking directly to the speaker, using the person's name and the pronoun "you," not "he" or "she." If someone says, "She said that...," intervene as promptly and respectfully as possible and say to the reviewer, "Talk to Betty...Say you." This is very important. The person whose turn is being reviewed will have a totally different feeling when talked to, instead of about.

Note: Remember that the review is optional and is most effective when used occasionally, not as a part of every circle.

ICE BREAKERS

Launching the Group
Introductions and Ground Rules

Procedure:

Begin by welcoming the students and briefly explaining the purpose of the group. For example, you might say:

Twice a year, I lead a series of group counseling sessions devoted to the subject of peer relations (communication, self-concept, racial issues, etc.). I want to welcome you to the first of those. You are here because you expressed an interest in getting together with other students to develop a greater understanding of yourselves and each other and perhaps improve your social and interpersonal skills. These are important subjects, but that doesn't mean that we have to be serious all of the time. We will have six 1-hour sessions together, and I hope that each of them will be enjoyable as well as productive. Let's begin by getting to know a little about each other, and by establishing some ground rules for our meetings.

Ask the students to pair up and spend 5-8 minutes interviewing their partners. Besides exchanging names, suggest that they ask each other these questions:

—What is your favorite subject at school?

—What hobbies, sports, or other activities are you involved in?

—What is one question you have about peer relations (self-concept, communication, racial issues, etc.)?

—How do you hope to benefit from attending this group?

Objectives:

Group members will:
—become acquainted with each other.
—understand the purpose of the group.
—describe rules to help the group function effectively.

Materials:

chart paper and markers

Write the questions on the board or chart so that the students can refer to them. Tell the students to listen carefully so that they can introduce their partners to the group later in the session.

Reconvene the group and have the students take turns introducing their partners. As the students briefly summarize what they learned about each other, make two lists on chart paper — one labeled *Questions*, and other *Expected Benefits*. Keep these lists and post them before each meeting. Refer to the lists at appropriate points during subsequent sessions, checking off items covered, questions answered, and benefits accrued.

Following the introductions, spend some time establishing ground rules for the group. Ask the students to think of behaviors that will help the group function well and therefore should be part of every session. Keep the list short, but try to include these items in one form or another:

- Listen to each other
- Don't use put-downs of any kind
- Everything said in the group stays in the group.

Save the rules list and display it during each session. Conclude by discussing how students can obtain maximum benefits from the group.

Discussion Questions:

1. What are some added things we can do to help each other get the most from this group?
2. When you feel shy about sharing your thoughts, what can the rest of us do to help you feel comfortable?
3. What could happen in the group if we allowed put-downs — even joking ones?
4. How do you think trust develops in a group?
5. If you disagree with what someone says, how can you express your own ideas without seeming to put down the other person?
6. What are some good communication behaviors that will help us in this group?

The Warm-up Wave!
Sentence Completion Exercises

Objectives:
Group members will:
— spontaneously complete sentences related to the group theme.
— get to know each other and the purpose of the group.

Materials:
board or chart paper

Procedure:
Pick a sentence starter related to the theme of the group and write it on the board or chart. As a way of opening the session, "send" the starter quickly around the group like a wave. Have each person in turn rise, tack an ending on the sentence, and sit back down. At times you might want to send the same starter around two or three times. Or begin a second starter immediately after the first one passes the last person in the group.

Self-concept
- I am proud because I...
- My favorite leisure activity is...
- When I'm bored, I...
- Something I do very well is...
- One of my biggest achievements is...
- My family counts on me to...
- Something I spend too much time doing is...
- An area in which I'm improving is...
- If I could change one thing about my appearance it would be...
- One of my best features is...

Communication
- When I want attention, I...
- Speaking in front of a group is...
- A person who always listens to me is...
- Communicating is hard because...
- Non-English speakers should...
- Learning a second language is...
- I usually start a conversation by...
- If I don't understand what someone is saying, I...
- I am good/bad at following directions because...
- One way I could improve my communication is...

Peer Relations
- A true friend never...
- One thing I look for in a friend is...
- The best way to meet people is...
- When I disagree with the crowd, I...
- I handle peer pressure by...
- Friends always let friends...
- I feel uncomfortable around kids who...
- I feel relaxed around kids who...
- When I'm totally myself, I...
- An issue I have with the opposite sex is...

Conflict Management
- When I'm angry at someone, I usually...
- When I disagree with someone, I...
- The way I feel about conflict is...
- When someone yells at me, I...
- People have disagreements because...
- When conflicts turn violent it's because...
- The best way to reduce violence is to...
- To be a better conflict manager, I need to...
- When I'm around people who are fighting, I want to...
- What TV teaches us about conflict is...

Succeeding in School
- My best/worst subject is...
- The thing I most look forward to at school is...
- A school rule I think should be changed is...
- The job of the counselor is to...
- Good teachers always...
- When I'm confused about something, I...
- The way to get good grades is to...
- Grades are important because...
- The best/worst thing that ever happened to me in school was...
- When I graduate I'm going to...

Changing Family Groups
- I feel that divorce is...
- The most important thing about families is...
- What I miss most is...
- The hardest thing to accept is...
- I appreciate my mother/father for...
- I depend on my family for...
- Change is hard because...
- I wish my mother/father wouldn't...
- When I get married, I...
- The ideal family is one that...

Cultural/Racial Issues
- A solution to racial problems is...
- I wish racial/ethnic groups would...
- As a member of a minority group, I...
- If I were part of a minority group, I'd...
- Sometimes I just can't tolerate...
- The problem with mixed marriages is...
- To solve the gang problem, we should...
- What Whites need to know about Blacks is...
- What Blacks need to know about Whites is...
- What Whites need to know about Latinos is...

Social/Sexual Harassment
- To be popular, a girl/boy has to...
- Girls are better than boys at...
- Boys are better than girls at...
- What males don't understand about females is...
- What females don't understand about males is...
- Sexual harassment would disappear if...
- The first thing a person who is harassed should do is...
- People who sexually harass other people are after...
- To protect themselves against harassment, girls/boys should...
- A way I resist peer pressure is...

Fool the Finders

A Warm-up Game

Objectives:
Group members will:
—learn each other's names.
—become energized and comfortable with one another.

Materials:
three or four marbles, rocks, or other small objects

Procedure:

First, make sure the group is seated in a circle. Then, choose two members of the group to be the "finders." Ask them to come into the center of the circle and close their eyes.

While the finders have their eyes closed, distribute the marbles, rocks, or other objects to members of the circle.

Have the finders open their eyes. Explain that the object of the game <u>for</u> <u>finders</u> is to locate the objects; the object of the game <u>for</u> <u>circle members</u> is to avoid being caught with an object in hand. In your own words, explain:

As circle members, you must pass — or pretend to pass — the objects around the circle without allowing the finders to see exactly what is happening. Finders, you must watch closely. When you think you know who has an object, call out that person's name. You may <u>not</u> point or refer to a person in any way other than by name. If you are correct, the person you "catch" will replace you in the center of the circle.

Continue playing until most students have had a turn being finder, or until the group begins to tire of the game.

Just Say It — Graffiti Style!
Individual Comments and Discussion

Objectives:
Group members will:
— freely express their ideas concerning a specific topic.
— discuss the individual ideas expressed and how those affect the group itself.

Note: Use this activity when a group is first getting started, to stimulate thinking about the group's specific purpose. Once the group is underway, use it when interaction appears to be getting bogged down, or when the students seem "stuck."

Materials:
a long sheet of butcher paper or large piece of newsprint or tag board; colored marking pens; masking tape

Procedure:
Tape the sheet of butcher paper to a bulletin board or wall. At the top, write a provocative phrase likely to generate ideas in keeping with the purpose of your group. For example:

- The hardest thing about relationships is...
- Friendship is...
- To get along with others, you have to...
- The best thing about families is...
- Divorce is hard because...
- Teachers are...
- To succeed in school, you have to...
- Self-esteem is...
- Girls are...
- Boys are...
- People argue and fight because...
- A question I have about this group is...
- To improve this group, I think we should...

Give the students a few minutes to think silently about their responses. Then, have two or three students at a time approach the mural and record their contributions.

Leave the mural up throughout the current session and as many more as you desire. Tell the students that they may quietly get up and add to the mural at any time.

When most of the students have contributed to the graffiti mural, spend some time talking about the results. Point out that the mural is like a mental map of the group's collective ideas about the topic. Encourage members to expand on that map through elaboration, sharing, and discussion.

Discussion Questions:

1. What similarities and differences do you see in our contributions?

2. Which graffiti entries do you agree with? ...disagree with?

3. Which entry do you have a question about?

4. Do any of the ideas tell us how we can work together better as a group? Which ones, and what do they suggest?

Something You Wouldn't Know...
A Warm-up Activity

Procedure:

Write this topic on the board or chart:

Something You Wouldn't Know About Me Unless I Told You

In your own words, say to the students:

We've already started getting to know each other better in this group. And with each meeting, I hope that we will become better and better acquainted — with each other's ideas, feelings, experiences, hopes, and concerns. However, just for the fun of it today, let's tell each other something that wouldn't normally come up in a group like this. When it's your turn, state your name. Then, think of something unusual, funny, offbeat, or peculiar to tell us. For instance, maybe you like to invent things, collect old mystery books, sleep with your pet iguana, or read the dictionary for fun. Perhaps you have a famous relative, know a foolproof cure for hiccups, or sing with gusto when you're alone. You can tell us just about anything, as long as it's something we probably wouldn't learn otherwise.

Begin the process by stating *your* name and telling something about yourself. Model the desired spirit by sharing something light and humorous. Then, go around the group and give each student an opportunity to speak.

If time permits, invite volunteers to prove their listening skills by repeating the names of people in the group and restating the information those people shared.

Objectives:

Group members will:
—learn each other's names.
—share something unusual about themselves.

Materials:

board or chart paper

The Same, But Different
A Warm-up Activity

Objectives:
Group members will:
— describe the unique features of a chosen object.
— relate the concept of "same, but different" to members of the group.

Materials:
a collection of objects wherein each object is unique, but all objects belong to the same category (e.g., flowers, stones, marbles, nuts, oranges, apples, bananas)

Procedure:
Pass the collection around the group and have each person select one object, briefly explaining to the group why that particular choice was made. You might want to go first, to model the process. Say something like:

I chose this flower because of its warm color, and because it is just starting to open — like we are in this group.

If you choose a category in which the objects are *very* similar (oranges, apples, etc.), have the students take a few moments to become familiar with their item before putting it back in the container it came from. Then, place all of the objects in the center of the group. Challenge the students to reach into the collection and choose the same object again. Ask them what distinguishing features they used to identify their object. Relate the concept of "the same but different" to similarities and uniquenesses in the group.

Discussion Questions:
1. In what ways are we the same, but different?

2. What caused these objects to become unique? What caused each of us to develop uniquely?

3. Which would you like to learn more about in this group, the similarities between us or the differences? Why?

Setting My Counselor Straight
A Warm-up Activity

Objectives:
Group members will:
—become familiar with the role of the counselor
—enjoy a relaxing mixer with the group.

Materials:
one copy of the experience sheet, "I Can Set My Counselor Straight!" for each student

Procedure:
Announce that group members are going to compete in a game. Distribute the experience sheets and read the directions with the students. Then, in your own words, explain:

When I say "go," begin unscrambling the words. There is no time limit. You may keep working until someone calls out "I Can Set My Counselor Straight." Then, everyone must stop while I check the person's sheet. If every item is correct, that person wins. If anything — including spelling — is incorrect, I will signal you to keep working. We will continue this way until someone gets every item right.

Signal the start of play.

Answer Key

1. goals
2. listens
3. skills
4. self-esteem
5. decisions
6. questions
7. schedule
8. grades
9. conflict
10. qualities
11. activities
12. learn
13. myself
14. stress
15. trust

I Can Set My Counselor Straight!
Student Experience Sheet

Directions: Straighten out the mixed-up words in each sentence. When you have them all, call out "I Can Set My Counselor Straight!"

1. My counselor helps me set _____ .
   _{aolgs}

2. My counselor _____ if I have a problem.
   _{tlsensi}

3. My counselor helps me learn _____ that improve my relationships.
   _{lkilss}

4. My counselor helps build my _____ .
   _{fsle-etemes}

5. My counselor helps me learn to make _____ .
   _{isodcines}

6. My counselor answers _____ my parents have about school.
   _{inoestsuq}

7. My counselor helps me arrange my _____ .
   _{dceuhles}

8. My counselor is concerned about my _____ in school.
   _{adegsr}

9. My counselor can help me settle a _____ with another student.
   _{fcnloitc}

10. My counselor points out my positive _____ to me.
    _{ealiqtisu}

11. My counselor can help me decide which _____ to participate in.
    _{vicaittise}

12. My counselor helps me figure out how I _____ best.
    _{ranle}

13. My counselor helps me understand _____ better.
    _{eyslmf}

14. My counselor teaches me how to handle _____ .
    _{stsrse}

15. My counselor may turn out to be someone I can _____ .
    _{urstt}

Here Comes Another Wave!
More Sentence Completion Exercises

Objectives:
Group members will:
—get to know each other's values and preferences.

Materials:
board or chart paper

Procedure:
Pick one of the incomplete sentences below and write it on the board or chart. As a way of opening the session, "send" the sentence quickly around the group like a wave. Have each person in turn rise, complete the sentence, and sit back down. Emphasize that each person's answer must have two parts:

1. the name of the item chosen
2. a "because" statement.

If the group is enjoying the exercise, try starting a second sentence as soon as the wave passes the last person in the group.

- If I were an animal, I'd be.... because...
- If I were a city, I'd be.... because...
- If I were a tree, I'd be.... because...
- If I were a TV show, I'd be.... because...
- If I were a tool, I'd be.... because...
- If I were a piece of furniture, I'd be.... because...
- If I were a musical instrument, I'd be.... because...
- If I were a song, I'd be.... because...
- If I were a book, I'd be... because...
- If I were a car, I'd be.... because...
- If I were a building, I'd be.... because...
- If I were a food, I'd be.... because...
- If I were a game, I'd be.... because...
- If I were an actor, I'd be.... because...
- If I were a bird, I'd be.... because...
- If I were an insect, I'd be.... because...
- If I were a fish, I'd be.... because...
- If I were a flower, I'd be.... because...
- If I were a color, I'd be.... because...
- If I were a movie, I'd be.... because...
- If I were a sport, I'd be.... because...
- If I were a street, I'd be.... because...
- If I were gift, I'd be.... because...
- If I were a musical group, I'd be.... because...
- If I were a another person, I'd be... because...

A Secret Wish I Have
A Sharing Circle

Objectives:
Group members will:

—get to know each other better.
—feel relaxed in the group.

Introduce the Topic:
The topic for today's circle is, "A Secret Wish I Have." We all have wishes that we daydream about. We imagine ourselves being or doing something and then we wish that we could make the image come true. You've probably wished over birthday candles, and maybe you've made a wish while throwing a penny into a fountain. Wishing is fun.

Tell us something that you've wished for. Maybe you've wished for a new outfit, some athletic equipment, a trip to a big amusement park, or a visit from someone you haven't seen for a long time. Perhaps you've wished that you could be a famous actor or singer, or perform so well in football or basketball that all the big colleges tried to recruit you. Secretly, you may wish to grow taller and become a model, or to someday own your own business. You might also have wished for something like peace in the world, an end to violence in our community, or freedom from hunger for all people. Close your eyes for a moment and let your mind explore our topic, "A Secret Wish I Have."

Discussion Questions:
1. Why is wishing important?
2. What would life by like without wishes and dreams?
3. What are some things you can do to make wishes come true?

One of My Favorite Possessions
A Sharing Circle

Objectives:
Group members will:
—become better acquainted with one another.
—feel relaxed in the group.

Introduce the Topic:
Our topic for today is, "One of My Favorite Possessions." You probably own several things that are special to you. You may have had some of these possessions since you were very young, and you may have acquired others more recently. Tell us about one thing you own that you really treasure, and tell us why this item means so much to you. Someone you care for very much may have given it to you, or you may have done extra chores to earn the money to buy it. Your favorite item could be a photograph, book, piece of jewelry, game, or a card that you received from someone. It could be something you wear, play with, work with, or decorate your room with. Think about it for a moment. The topic is, "One of My Favorite Possessions."

Discussion Questions:
1. What is it that makes certain things important to us?
2. Why do we buy souvenirs when we go to new places?
3. Do you think most people place too much importance on possessions? Why or why not?

The Best News I Could Get Right Now
A Sharing Circle

Objectives:
Group members will:
—become better acquainted with one another.
—feel comfortable in the group.

Introduce the Topic:
Today's topic is, "The Best News I Could Get Right Now." If you think about it for a moment or so, you can probably come up with a piece of news or information that, if you heard it this very minute, would make you very happy. Maybe you entered a contest and are waiting to hear if you won, or perhaps you are hoping to receive a particular message from a friend, teacher, or relative. Your good news could be about you, or someone you know, or it could involve an important local, state, national, or world event. It might be earth-shattering news, or it might be something simple and personal. If someone walked through the door right now with a note for you, what would it say? The topic is, "The Best News I Could Get Right Now."

Discussion Questions:
1. What kinds of feelings do you experience when you get extremely good news? ...when you are waiting for news?

2. What are *expectations* and how do you feel when your expectations are met? ...not met?

3. If I asked you to set a goal for yourself to help you receive the good news you want, what would your goal be?

SELF-CONCEPT

How We See Ourselves
Self-Assessment, Sharing, and Discussion

Objectives:
Group members will:
— rate the degree to which they possess specific qualities/characteristics.
— represent their self-concept pictorially or in words.
— describe how self-concept affects daily living.

Materials:
one copy of the experience sheet, "Looking at Me" for each student; fine- and medium-point colored markers for students who choose to draw an image of themselves

Procedure:
Begin with a brief discussion about self-concept. Remind the students that self-concept is like looking in the mirror, except that the image we have depends more on our thoughts and conclusions about ourselves than it does on the physical mechanisms involved in sight. Point out that people often see themselves quite differently than others see them.

Distribute the experience sheets and briefly review the directions. Give the students about 15 minutes to complete the sheet. Make colored marking pens available to students who wish to draw pictures of themselves instead of writing paragraphs.

If the group is large, have the students form smaller groupings (three to five) and share their self-assessments and drawings/paragraphs. If the group is small, complete this part of the activity as a total group. Emphasize that all sharing is voluntary, and that students may keep any or all parts of the experience sheet confidential if they choose.

Conclude the activity by facilitating further discussion about self-concept.

Discussion Questions:

1. Did you learn anything about yourself from this activity that surprised you? What was it?

2. What strengths did your self-assessment reveal?

3. What qualities would you like to develop more of?

4. What qualities would you like to reduce or eliminate?

5. What qualities or concerns did you discover you have in common with other members of the group?

6. How does self-concept affect our performance at school? ...our relations with other people? ...our outlook on life and the future?

Looking at Me
Self-Assessment

Read through the list of characteristics, below. Decide how well each characteristic fits YOU. Be honest. If you are unsure about an item, ask yourself how others see you. Circle the point on the scale that describes you best.

                Most of the time   **Average**   **Almost never**

1. Well-liked
2. Good looking
3. Intelligent
4. Popular
5. Athletic
6. Appreciated
7. Talented
8. Happy
9. Worried
10. Relaxed
11. Caring
12. Strong
13. Unique
14. Assertive
15. Enthusiastic
16. Energetic
17. Tense
18. Dependable
19. A good friend
20. Boring
21. Tough
22. Confident
23. Unhappy
24. Creative
25. A leader
26. Friendly
27. Helpful
28. Responsible
29. Fun
30. Angry
31. Honest
32. Successful
33. A loner
34. Shy
35. Generous

On the other side of this paper, draw a picture or write a paragraph that describes your thoughts and feelings about yourself.

Group Activities for Counselors   Self-Concept

Looking at Self-Esteem
True-False Test and Discussion

Objectives:
Group members will:
—assess their beliefs about self-esteem.
—define self-esteem and describe how it develops.
—identify specific ways of strengthening their own self-esteem.

Materials:
one copy of "The Truth About Self-Esteem" for each student

Procedure:
Distribute the experience sheets and give the students a few minutes to complete them. If you are working with younger students, read each item aloud while the students read silently along. Clarify the meaning of the items, as necessary.

When the students have finished making their choices, go back through the items, one at a time, and discuss them. Ask for a show of hands from students who think the statement is true, and from those who think it is false. Answer questions and encourage the students to challenge and debate one another. In the course of the discussion, make these (and other) points about self-esteem.

- Our self-esteem is comprised of the feelings and opinions we have about ourselves.

- Self-esteem begins to form at a very young age.

- A baby learns to value itself based on how much it is valued by others. Children draw conclusions about the opinions and judgments that adults have of them. They *internalize* those judgments and make them their own.

- Virtually every decision we make and every action we take in life is based on our thoughts and beliefs about ourselves.

- Our thoughts and beliefs about ourselves are reflected in our "self-talk," which constantly reinforces or modifies the state of our self-esteem.

- All people make mistakes and all people occasionally fail. These are the prices of learning and growth. Unfortunately, too many people focus on their shortcomings, while ignoring their strengths and accomplishments.

- One way for young people to build self-esteem is to realize that they are unique in the history of the world. No other human being has ever been exactly like they are.

- Another way for young people to build self-esteem is to acquire skills and competencies and to give themselves credit (and ask for credit from others) for every increment of growth.

- A third way to build self-esteem is to deliberately and systematically eliminate negative self-talk and replace it with positive self-talk.

Discussion Questions:

1. What is self-esteem?

2. Why is it important to build positive self-esteem?

3. What is self-talk and where does it come from?

4. What can you do when you catch yourself using negative self-talk?

5. What kinds of choices are affected by self-esteem?

6. What decisions have you made recently that would have been different if your self-esteem had been more positive?

Variation:

Read selected items from the experience sheet and/or write them on the board or a chart. Discuss each item with the group as a whole. (This approach is recommended for use with younger students.)

The Truth About Self-Esteem

Experience Sheet

Read each item and decide if you think the statement is true or false. Circle your answer.

T F 1. All human beings are worthwhile.

T F 2. A baby learns to feel worthwhile, or not worthwhile, by the way it is treated.

T F 3. Smart people and good looking people almost always have high self-esteem.

T F 4. If you like yourself, others will think you're conceited.

T F 5. Students who feel good about themselves don't do any better in school than students who feel bad about themselves.

T F 6. If you are told frequently that you are incapable of doing something, you will eventually doubt your ability to do it.

T F 7. When you feel worthwhile, you don't need to act phoney toward others, or pretend to be something you're not.

T F 8. Most people think they're great.

T F 9. How you feel about yourself affects everything you do in life.

T F 10. The opinions others have about us never become our opinions about ourselves.

T F 11. You can learn to like yourself even if you think others don't like you.

T F 12. If you try hard enough, you can get everyone to like you.

T F 13. People tend to like people who like themselves.

T F 14. Some people refuse to try new things because they fear failure.

T F 15. If you really want to like yourself, you must become perfect at everything you do that is important to you.

T F 16. The words you say to yourself about your own worth determine how you feel about yourself.

T F 17. If you tell yourself you are going to fail at something, you're more likely to fail.

T F 18. Some people are completely worthless.

T F 19. Everyone makes mistakes.

T F 20. You become what you think you are.

T F 21. There are only a few people in the world exactly like you.

T F 22. There is nothing to be learned from making a mistake.

T F 23. Feeling like a terrible person probably means you are a terrible person.

T F 24. You are special because there is no one else like you in the world.

T F 25. People who brag a lot about their accomplishments often have low self-esteem.

T F 26. You don't have to be perfect to be a worthwhile person. You only have to be yourself.

T F 27. Every single person has some things to be proud of.

T F 28. People who feel good about themselves are conceited.

T F 29. Every person has talents and abilities that can be developed.

T F 30. Once a failure, always a failure.

T F 31. It's silly to think and say nice things to yourself.

T F 32. If you act proud of your accomplishments, no one will like you.

Developing Metaphor Names
Individual Creativity and Group Discussion

Procedure:
Begin the activity by focusing on the importance of names. Make these points:

- Most of us have no choice about our name — it is selected before or at the time of our birth.
- Our name is as much a part of us as our eyes, teeth, or hands. We can't see or touch it, but it is always there.
- Our name represents *everything* that is known about us. Just like the name *Disney* creates a mental image of hundreds of movies, videos, cartoon characters and recreational acres, our name creates an image that encompasses our totality.
- Some of us don't like our names.

Go around the group and ask the students to tell the group something about their name: who they were named after; their middle name; a problem their name causes; why their parents picked that name; etc.

Next, ask the group: *How many of us are happy with our names?*

Objectives:
Group members will:

—identify an aspect of their self-concept that they wish to project.
—create a name to represent that aspect.
—describe the power and significance of names.

Materials:
large tag board strips; colored marking pens; masking tape

Tell the students that since names are so important, they are going to have an opportunity to create their own name — a *metaphor* name.

Explain that a metaphor name stands for something about the person who bears it. It creates a mental picture that is in keeping with some aspect of that person's self-concept. Give several examples: Quiet River, Soaring Eagle, Light Sleeper; Digital Dancer; Chameleon Child.

Urge the students to create a name that truly represents them. Give them plenty of time to do this. Encourage students who like to bounce their ideas off of others to interact quietly.

Note: If a majority of students would like to have additional time to develop a name, postpone the remainder of the activity until the next session.

Distribute the tag board and markers. Have the students write or print their metaphor name on the strip, adding a symbol or logo if they wish. Then have them tape the strip so that it hangs from the front of their desk (or is displayed in some other visible location).

Go around the group and have each member explain the significance of his/her metaphor name and how it was developed. Ask each student if she or he would like to be addressed by that name in the group. Allow those students who wish, to leave their name tags displayed throughout the remainder of the sessions. Lead a culminating discussion.

Discussion Questions:

1. How can a name help or hurt our self-concept?

2. Would you ever consider changing your name? Why or why not?

3. What other things about yourself would you like to change? Would they be harder or easier to change than your name?

4. If you want to project the image of your metaphor name, in what other ways can you do it?

5. What have you learned about self-concept from this activity?

Variation:

Instead of tag board strips, distribute art paper. In addition to writing their metaphor names, have the students draw pictures of themselves that illustrate the significance of those names.

In the Middle

Discussions in Inner-Outer Circles

Objectives:
Group members will:
—define self-esteem.
—discuss specific questions about self-esteem.

Materials:
board or chart paper

Procedure:
Begin by reminding the students of the meaning of *self-esteem*. If the group has not already defined the term, take a few minutes to do so.

Have the group count off by two's. Have the one's move their chairs together to form a circle and sit facing each other. Have the two's form a circle around the outside, facing in.

Pick a question from the list on the opposite page, and write it on the board or chart paper. Direct the students in the inner circle to discuss the topic; have the students in the outer circle listen and be prepared to comment or ask questions at the end of the discussion period. Allow at least 5 minutes.

Call time and invite the students in the outside circle to comment. Be sure that they direct their comments to the students in the inner circle, not to you. When they have finished commenting, give the inner circle 1-2 minutes to respond.

Have the students switch places (inner circle becoming outer circle) and repeat the process, using a new question from the list.

Questions:

—How important is self-esteem?

—How does low self-esteem affects a person's ability to resolve conflict?

—How does self-esteem help or hurt when a person is faced with a tough subject or assignment?

—How is saying positive things about yourself different from bragging?

—How does having high self-esteem help a person cope with new situations or meet new people?

—What do you think parents should do to build the self-esteem of their children?

—What can a person do to improve his or her own self-esteem?

—What abilities and skills should a person try to develop that will also improve self-esteem?

Conclude with a general discussion involving everyone.

Discussion Questions:

1. What did you like about this process? What did you dislike?

2. What ideas did you hear about self-esteem that are particularly meaningful to you?

3. What good does it do to talk about self-esteem? How can talking about it help improve it?

Variation:

Place an empty chair in the inner circle. Explain that the empty chair is for individual students from the outer circle who have something they'd like to contribute to the discussion. Such students are to enter the circle, sit in the chair, wait until they have an opportunity to speak (without interrupting), say what they have to say, and then leave.

Four Concepts
Creative Self-Assessment and Discussion

Objectives:
Group members will:
- distinguish between how others see them and how they see themselves.
- distinguish between present self-concept and desired self-concept.

Materials:
one copy of the experience sheet, "Concepts of Me" for each student; fine- and medium-tip marking pens in various colors

Procedure:
Remind the students of the definition of self-concept. (You may wish to distinguish between self-*concept* and self-*esteem*. Self-concept is one's view of self; self-esteem is the value placed on that view.)

Distribute the experience sheets, and place the marking pens where the students can share them. Go over the directions printed on the sheet. Emphasize that the students may employ descriptive word lists, paragraph descriptions, illustrations, symbols — even poetry — to complete their four descriptions. Suggest they begin with quadrant 1, and do the rest in any sequence they wish.

Allow sufficient time for thinking and creativity. When the students have finished, have them read (or show) and explain their descriptions to the group. Facilitate discussion.

Discussion Questions:
1. Why do others see us differently than we see ourselves?
2. If you asked your best friend to describe you, which quadrant would his/her description match most closely? Why?
3. Which quadrants do you wish were more similar?
4. What can you do to bring those images closer together?

Concepts of Me
Experience Sheet

Your *self-concept* is how you *view* yourself. It is what you *think about* yourself. Other people also have a concept of you. In the spaces below, write or draw four descriptions (concepts) of you. Notice their similarities and differences.

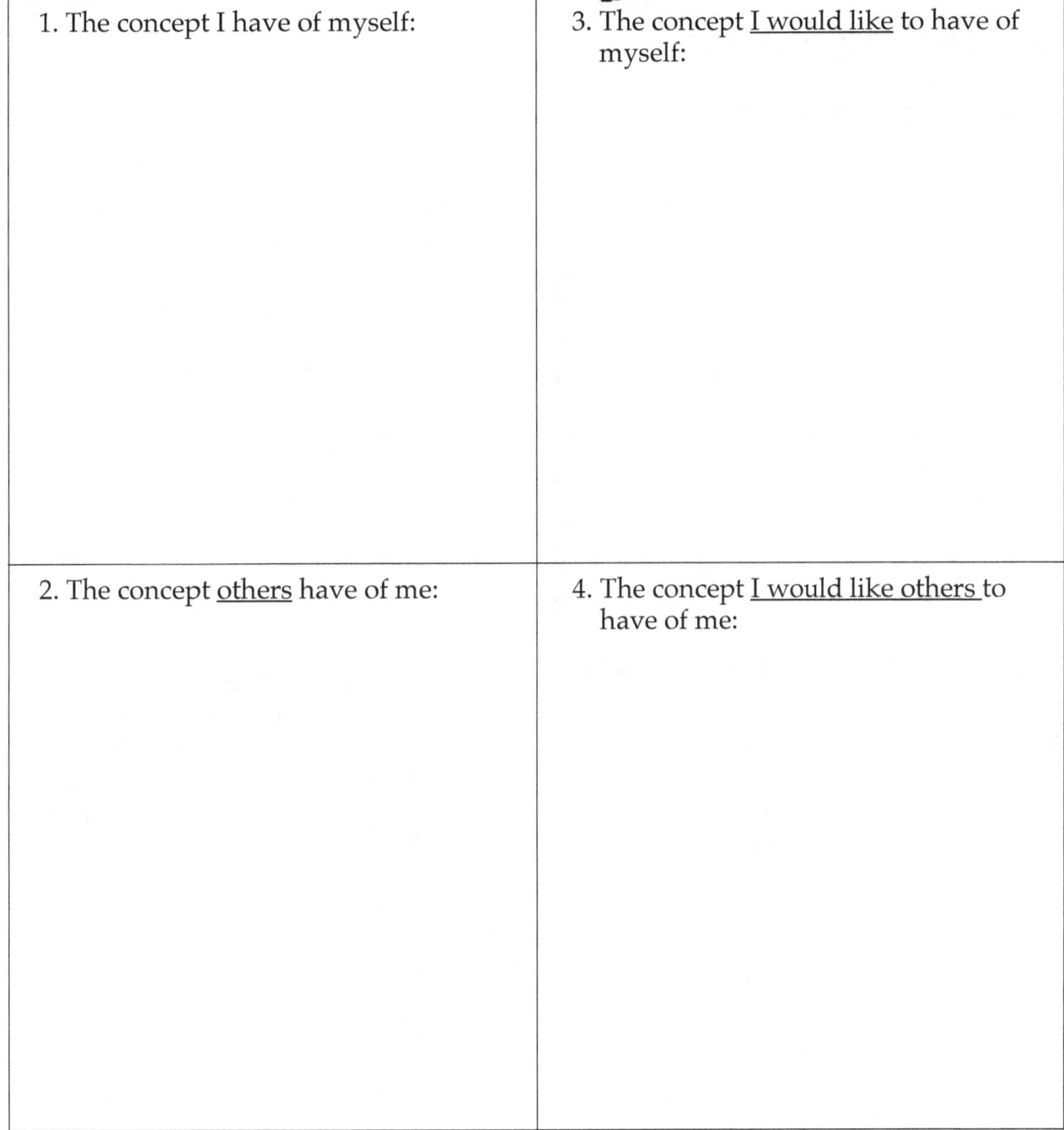

1. The concept I have of myself:	3. The concept <u>I would like</u> to have of myself:

2. The concept <u>others</u> have of me:	4. The concept <u>I would like others</u> to have of me:

SELF-CONCEPT — Group Activities for Counselors

Growing Pains
A Group Discussion

Objectives:
Group members will:

—identify social problems common to young people.
—associate typical situations with emotional responses.
—describe ways of resolving typical social problems.

Materials:
none

Procedure:
Read the following situations to the group, one at a time. Ask the questions listed and discuss each situation before going on to the next.

Note: In place of the following situations, you may substitute examples that are more relevant to problems occurring right now in your own school. However, should the group members know any of the students involved, do not allow them to mention names.

- Sandra's family doesn't have much money and she wears clothes that are old and out of style. She can't seem to make friends with the other girls in class. They ignore her and don't include her in any of their activities.

—What is Sandra's problem?
—How do you think Sandra feels?
—How would you feel if you were in a similar situation?
—Can Sandra do anything about her clothes?
—If you were in the class, how would you treat Sandra?

- Manny has been called into the principal's office for fighting. In the past, Manny has been a quiet student, but this year the kids are calling him names like "Fat Man," "Lard Face," and "The Whale."

—What is Manny's problem?
—How do you think Manny feels?
—How would you feel if you were in a similar situation?
—If you were in the class and were Manny's friend, what would you do?
—What do you think Manny should do?

- Off and on for several weeks, Lisa has been finding excuses not to dress for physical education class. First it's a cold, then a sore shoulder, and now a sprained ankle wrapped with an ace bandage. The P.E. teacher finally sends Lisa to talk with the counselor. Later that day, the counselor tells the teacher that Lisa is upset because several girls in class make fun of her appearance and lack of coordination. Sometimes the same girls are rude, push her, or call her "retard."

—*What is Lisa's problem?*
—*How do you think Lisa feels?*
—*How would you feel if you were in a similar situation?*
—*If you were in the class and were Lisa's friend, what would you do?*
—*What do you think Lisa should do?*

- Kevin is 12 years old. He is taller than the other boys his age, and his voice is beginning to change. One day, while giving a report in class, his voice suddenly drops and he lets out a couple of loud croaking sounds while trying to regain control of his speech. Everyone in class breaks out laughing. Even after the teacher quiets the students, they quietly giggle and snicker. No one listens to the rest of Kevin's report.

—*What is Kevin's problem?*
—*How do you think Kevin feels?*
—*How would you feel if you were in a similar situation?*
—*If you were in the class and were Kevin's friend, what would you do?*

When you have finished talking about the four example problems, move the discussion to real problems with which the students are dealing.

Discussion Questions:

1. Have you ever had a problem similar to any of the ones we talked about? If so, would you be willing to talk about it?

2. How do problems like this affect self-concept?

3. How can we build our self-concepts when circumstances like these are breaking them down?

4. Why do some students tease and harass other students?

5. Do you think students are more apt to tease and torment when they are alone or part of a group? Why?

Handling Discomfort
Experience Sheet and Discussion

Objectives:
Group members will:

—identify individual situations and personal characteristics that cause them discomfort.
—describe strategies for dealing with areas of discomfort.

Materials:
one copy of the experience sheet, "Things That Bother Me," for each student

Procedure:
Tell the students that they are going to have a chance to talk about ways of dealing with situations and problems that cause them particular discomfort.

Distribute the experience sheet and give the students a few minutes to complete it. Invite volunteers to share one or two items that they circled on their sheet. Model reflective listening, allowing the contributions of the students to generate discussion. Make these points:

- We are all bothered by different things because each of us is unique. We have different abilities, disabilities, likes, dislikes, perceptions and experiences.
- Everyone in the group is at the same stage of development, so we share common experiences and concerns.
- Talking about our discomforts and concerns can help us deal with them more effectively.

Discussion Questions:
1. How many of the things you marked on your list can you change?
2. In your opinion, how many kids are bothered by the same things you are?
3. What feelings do you have in connection with the things that bother you?
4. When you have a problem, how do you usually resolve it?
5. How can you handle the stress that is caused by your discomfort?

Things That Bother Me
Experience Sheet

Read the list carefully and put a check next to any problems that bother you. If you are having a problem that is *not* on the list, describe it at the bottom.

I am uncomfortable because I am...

1. ...shorter than the other kids.
2. ...taller than the other kids.
3. ...have a speech impairment.
4. ...lose my temper; get into fights.
5. ...don't like school.
6. ...have too much work to do at home.
7. ...timid or shy.
8. ...don't know how to act at parties.
9. ...disliked by other kids.
10. ...talked about behind my back by other kids.
11. ...teased by other kids.
12. ...afraid to try new things.
13. ...don't like my teacher.
14. ...afraid of someone at home.
15. ...too fat.
16. ...too thin.
17. ...not smart enough.
18. ...don't have anyone to talk to at home.
19. ...have no place to study at home.
20. ...have a disability.
21. ...don't read well.
22. ...don't understand math.
23. ...afraid to admit my mistakes.
24. ...don't have nice clothes.
25. ...hungry all the time.
26. ...chosen last for teams.
27. ...not having any fun at school.
28. ...disliked by my teacher.
29. ...have bad dreams.
30. ...lose things.
31. ...have almost no friends.
32.
33.
34.

Self-Concept · 47 · Group Activities for Counselors

My Greatest Asset
A Sharing Circle

Objectives:
Group members will:

—identify a personal strength.
—explain how the recognition of personal assets contributes to self-esteem.

Introduce the Topic:
Today's Sharing Circle topic is, "My Greatest Asset." Everyone has assets. In the financial world, our assets are property, stocks, cash — things that add to our wealth. Assets in our personal lives represent a different kind of wealth. They are the attributes we possess and the skills we've developed.

What is your greatest asset? Maybe it's your ability to speak a second language, your sense of humor, or your determination even in tough situations. It might be your loyalty, your ability to make others feel comfortable, or your sense of style. Maybe you are excellent at drawing, dancing, writing, computing, or solving math problems. Or perhaps you're good at listening, often hearing what others are feeling but not saying. Review some of the many assets you have, and choose the one you think is your greatest. Our topic is, "My Greatest Asset."

Discussion Questions:
1. Why is it important to recognize our assets?

2. Which are more important, personal assets or financial assets? Why?

3. Why is it sometimes difficult to talk about ourselves positively?

Something I Hate to Do
A Sharing Circle

Objectives:
Group members will:

—describe an activity that they dislike.
—explore how values and attitudes determine our relative acceptance of an activity.

Introduce the Topic:
We all occasionally find ourselves doing something that we dislike. Today, we're going to have an opportunity to talk about times like this. Our topic is, "Something I Hate To Do."

What is one of your least favorite things to do? Maybe it's something you have to do on a regular basis, like clean your room, mow the lawn, or take a test. Or perhaps it's something that only happens once in awhile, like writing a term paper, visiting the dentist, moving to a new home, or giving a speech. I'm sure you can think of many things you don't like doing, but pick just one to share with us. The topic is, "Something I Hate to Do."

Discussion Questions:
1. What similarities did you notice in the things we hate to do?

2. When you're doing something you dislike, do you think your attitude affects how well you perform? What about your values?

3. What made you decide to have such strong feelings about the thing you shared?

A Significant Event in My Life
A Sharing Circle

Objectives:
Group members will:

—identify a life event that strongly affected them.
—explain how and why they attach significance to events.

Introduce the Topic:
Today's circle topic is, "A Significant Event in My Life." There are many kinds of events that hold places of importance in our memories. What is one of the most significant that you can recall? It could be an achievement, such as winning an academic or athletic competition or mastering a skill, or it could be a personal triumph, such as gaining control of a habit. Your significant event might be a move you made to a new city or school. Or it might be a negative event, such as the death of a pet or a divorce in the family. Think of one event in your life that you would like to share. Tell us what it was and why it holds a position of prominence in your memory. Our topic is, "A Significant Event in My Life."

Discussion Questions:
1. Who decides how much significance an event has?
2. What determines an event's relative importance?
3. How do you think you will feel in five or ten years about events that are significant to you now?
4. How do negative events become significant? Don't we just want to forget them?

COMMUNICATION

Experiencing Communication Blocks
Game and Discussion

Procedure:
Ask the students to count off by two's. Have the 1's place their chairs (or desks) in a circle facing out, leaving as much space as possible between chairs.

Ask the 2's to meet with you briefly. Give each of the 2's a copy of the experience sheet. Tell them that you will be giving them directions during the activity. When you call out a number, they are to demonstrate the behavior that corresponds to that number on the sheet. For example, when you call out "#7," they are to start giving lots of advice to their partner. Instruct them to keep the sheet in hand, but not to show it to their partner.

Have the 2's take their chairs and sit down facing the 1's, forming pairs. (If a student is left over, ask that student to be an observer during the first half of the activity.)

Write the following topic of the board:

> "What I Hope to Get Out of
>
> Being in This Group"

Objectives:
Group members will:

— demonstrate seven common communication blocks.
— describe how non-listening behaviors block communication.
— identify good listening behaviors.

Materials:
one copy of the experience sheet, "Seven Blocks to Communication" for each student

Instruct the 1's to start talking to their partners about the topic. Tell the 2's to demonstrate #1 on their sheet. Allow the students to interact for about 1 minute. Then have the 2's get up, move to the right and sit down in front of a new partner.

Again, tell the 1's to begin talking about the topic. Tell the 2's to demonstrate #3 on their sheet. Allow another minute of interaction.

Repeat the process twice more, with the 2's demonstrating #5 and #7.

In the second half of the activity, ask the 2's to give their experience sheets to the 1's and move to the inside of the circle. Repeat the process three more times, with the 2's discussing the topic while the 1's rotate around the circle and demonstrate #2, #4, and #6 from the sheet.

Note: If you have an uneven number of students, choose a new observer during the second half, so that the first observer can participate in the remainder of the activity.

Lead a follow-up discussion. Before the students leave, be sure that everyone has a copy of the experience sheet.

Discussion Questions:

1. What did the observers see that they would like to comment on?

2. How did you feel when you were trying to talk and your partner was fidgeting? ...interrupting? ...looking around? ...criticizing? ...asking questions? ...disagreeing? ...giving advice?

3. How did you feel when you were demonstrating non-listening behaviors?

4. Which of these behaviors do you think are most common?

5. Why are they called "blocks to communication?"

6. How can you avoid using communication blocks?

7. What does a good listener do?

Seven Blocks to Communication
Experience Sheet

Here are seven things **NOT** to do when you want to communicate well. They block communication in a number of ways. They prove that you are <u>not listening</u>.

> **#1 Fidget.** Play with your hair and clothes, twiddle your fingers, swing your leg, or tap your foot.
>
> **#2 Don't look at your partner.** Look around the room, at the clock, at your hands, or anywhere else. Don't have eye contact with your partner.
>
> **#3 Interrupt.** Every time your partner starts talking, break in with a question or a statement.
>
> **#4 Ask questions.** Lots of them. Every time your partner starts talking, ask a question, such as, "Why did you do that?" or "Why do you feel that way?"
>
> **#5 Criticize.** Tell your partner all the things that are wrong with his or her ideas, clothes, hair, friends, etc.
>
> **#6 Disagree.** Every time your partner says something, disagree. Tell your partner that he or she is wrong.
>
> **#7 Give advice.** Every time your partner starts talking, make a suggestion. Pretend to know a lot more than your partner does.

Diagrams Plus!
Showing How Communication Works

Procedure:

Begin by asking the group: *When you have thoughts or feelings that you want to share with another person, how do you usually convey them?*

The students will probably answer that they use words or language to convey their thoughts and feelings. Facilitate a discussion about the nature of communication, helping the students to recognize the role and importance of nonverbal as well as verbal communication. At some point, introduce the concept of *coding*. In your own words, explain:

Communication is a process in which one person sends a message to another person. Thoughts and feelings can't be <u>given</u> to anyone, so <u>codes</u> and <u>signals</u> are used to represent them. The most common type of code consists of words. Signals are usually gestures, body movements, and facial expressions.

Ask the students to think back over their day (or previous evening) and to think of — and write down — one communication exchange that they had with another person. Give them an example from your own experience, such as:

The counselor asks the secretary, "How many students are waiting to see me?" The secretary takes a quick look around the room and answers, "Only one. The rest are waiting for the principal."

Objectives:
Group members will:

— describe what happens in the communication process.
— demonstrate how verbal codes and nonverbal signals are used to convey messages.
— diagram examples of verbal and nonverbal exchanges between two people.

Materials:
board or chart paper

Allow a couple of minutes for thinking and writing. Then, on the board or chart paper, diagram the exchange you used as your example.

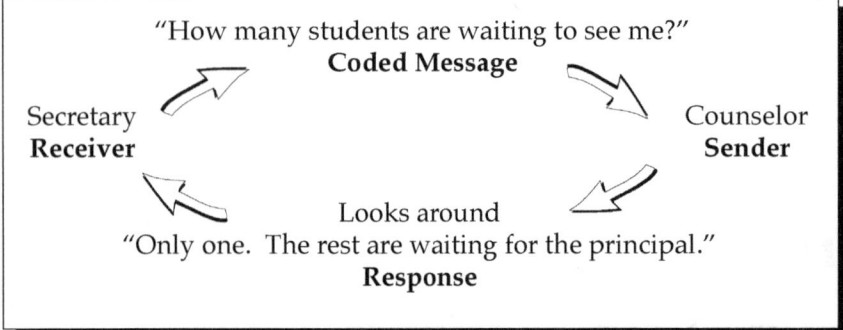

Point out that the diagram shows what happens when two people communicate. Make sure everyone understands the concepts of *sender*, *receiver*, *code*, *message*, and *response*.

Ask volunteers to share the communication exchanges they wrote down. One at a time, have them approach the board and diagram the exchanges. Encourage the group to be supportive and helpful during this process, coaching as necessary.

If the students have difficulty grasping the idea, read additional examples from the following list. Ask individual students to diagram them (with help from the group).

- Manny says excitedly to Victor, "I used the computer lab today. That new math program is great." Victor shrugs and says, "Yeah, so?"

- Linda asks her Mom, "Is it okay if I go to Lia's after school today?" Mom frowns and answers, "When do you plan to practice your violin?"

- Dave asks Clifford, "Did you win your game on Saturday?" Clifford frowns and turns both thumbs down.

- The teacher announces, "We will have a quiz on this chapter tomorrow." Thirty groans chorus loudly in response.

- Debbie shakes her head and says to John, "I don't think I can give this report." John replies, "You seem worried."

- Myan giggles and jumps up and down. Watching her, Lisa says, "You sure seem happy. What happened to make you feel so good?"

Discuss each student example as it is diagramed. Include nonverbal behaviors in the diagrams. When all of the students have had an opportunity to try diagraming, facilitate a wrap-up discussion.

Discussion Questions:

1. When a person's words and actions don't match, which do you usually pay more attention to? Why?

2. What can you learn by looking at the person to whom you are speaking?

3. How do you feel when you say something to a person and get no response of any kind?

4. How can you improve your own communication?

5. What have you learned about communication from this activity?

Extension:

Have two students role play each example before it is diagramed. When debriefing, isolate verbal and nonverbal behaviors and discuss how they reinforce or contradict each other.

Here's What You Need to Know
A Listening Experiment

Procedure:
Tell the students that you are going to read three announcements to them and that, afterwards, they are to recall the information as accurately as possible. Suggest that they take notes, just as they would if they were hearing the announcement on the radio, TV, or at a meeting.

Read the following announcements slowly and clearly, but do not repeat them. After each announcement, give the students about 30 seconds to complete their notes. Then, ask the related questions.

- RAI Studios needs extras of all ages for the movie, "Golden Fields" which is being filmed here throughout the month of October. If you are interested, be among the first one-hundred people to arrive at the parking lot behind Raleigh's grocery store at the corner of Juniper street and 10th avenue tomorrow at 7:00 a.m. Shooting will last through the day, and every extra chosen will be paid a flat fee of $150. Children between twelve and eighteen must bring signed parental permission addressed to the studio, and children under twelve must be accompanied by an adult.

—*What is the name of the movie?*
—*What studio is making the movie?*
—*How will the extras be chosen?*
—*What is the pay?*
—*What special instructions were given for children?*

Objectives:
Group members will:

—test their ability to accurately capture and recall the details of announcements.
—describe how memory is used during listening and recall.
—describe how interest affects listening ability.

Materials:
paper and pencils

- A free session will explain the benefits of the Acme computer camp, a summer day camp for children in grades four through eight who want to learn about computers and five of the most popular software programs currently being used in homes and schools. Camp classes meet from 8:00 a.m. to 1:30 p.m., and all materials and equipment are provided. Anyone can attend the introductory session at 8:00 p.m. Wednesday, April 22nd in the Sunset Room of the Dobbs Hotel, 3030 Circle Drive. For more information, call 689-7000.

—What is the price of the introductory session?
—What is the price of the camp?
—What is the purpose of the introductory session?
—Who is the camp for?
—How many software programs are taught at the camp?
—Where is the introductory session being held?

- My house is at 3946 Taylor Ridge Road. To get there, walk west four blocks on Center Drive until you get to the high school. Turn left and go up the hill on Harvard Street. At the top of the hill, after the stop sign, Harvard Street turns into Taylor Ridge Road. Keep going south until you come to the first side street to the right. My house is the sixth one on the right.

—How many blocks do you walk on Center Drive?
—Where do you turn off Center Drive?
—What landmark is at the corner of Center Drive and Harvard Street?
—Where does Harvard Street turn into Taylor Ridge Road?
—What is the address on Taylor Ridge Road?

If time permits, allow volunteers to give directions to their home, a relative's home, or some other location (without mentioning the place by name), and then test the group using questions similar to those above.

Lead a culminating discussion, focusing on the role of memory in good listening.

Discussion Questions:

1. Which of the announcements was the hardest to recall?

2. Which was the easiest?

3. Did it help to take notes? Explain.

4. Were you aware of using your memory to store information until you could write it down? Describe how you did that.

5. Which announcement was the most interesting to you? How did interest affect your ability to recall the details?

Active Listening
Group Practice and Discussion

Procedure:

Ask for a volunteer to help you with a demonstration. Invite the student to sit down opposite you, making certain that all other members of the group can see.

Ask the student to start talking about a current problem or issue that s/he doesn't mind discussing in front of the group. Demonstrate active listening. (Reflect content and feelings, show interest and empathy, etc.) Continue until you have been able to offer the student six or eight active listening responses, or until the student stops talking (whichever comes first).

Ask the group: *What was I doing?*

Elicit the group's observations, ascertaining that your listening behavior had specific characteristics. Ask the students if they can describe those characteristics. Write notes on the board or chart paper, and begin building a model for active listening.

Ask the students to recall what happens during the communication process (as taught in the activity, "Diagrams Plus").

Objectives:

Group members will:

— explain how active listening fits within the communication process.
— practice formulating active listening responses in a group setting.

Materials:

board or chart paper

Review the concepts of Sender, Receiver, Message, Code, Signal, and Feedback/Response.

In your own words (and utilizing relevant notes from the board), relate active listening to the communications model:

When a person wants to talk to you — particularly about a problem or issue of some kind — the most effective way for you to listen is <u>actively</u>. In active listening, you paraphrase and feed back to the sender what you hear *the sender saying. If you notice feelings, you feed those back, too. For example, you might say, "You sound pretty upset about that" or "You seem confused about what to do." An active listening response lets the sender know that he or she has been heard and understood. This encourages the person to talk further about the problem. Usually, if your response is inaccurate, the sender will correct you. For example, the sender might say, "No, that's not exactly what I mean. Actually, I do know what to do, I'm just afraid to do it!" Active listening is an extremely useful communication skill, and anyone can learn it.*

Model several more examples of active listening responses. When you are sure that the students understand the process, engage them in practice.

Have the group move their chairs to form a semicircle or U-shape. Place a chair at the open end of the semicircle, facing in. Ask a volunteer to sit in the chair, face the person on the left end of semicircle, and begin talking about any issue or concern that s/he is willing to share. Tell the speaker to pause after a couple of sentences to give the listener an opportunity to respond.

Help the first listener formulate an active listening response. If the response is accurate (which you will know by the speaker's reaction), have the speaker turn to the second person in the semicircle and continue talking about the same issue. When the second listener gives an accurate response, have the speaker turn to the third speaker, and so on around the semicircle to the right. If the speaker resolves his/her issue before getting all the way around the semicircle, simply stop. If the speaker prefers to continue, have him/her return to the first person without breaking the process.

Repeat this process using additional volunteer speakers. Debrief the speaker and the listeners after each round, facilitating discussion.

Discussion Questions:

To the speaker:

1. How did you feel when you received an accurate active listening response?

2. When a response didn't quite capture what you were feeling or saying, what did you do?

3. Did active listening help you sort out your thoughts and feelings about this issue? How?

To the listeners:

1. What was easiest about active listening? What was hardest?

2. How did you feel when you were giving an active listening response?

3. What did you learn about your own listening behaviors from this exercise?

Variation:

Sit in the speaker's chair yourself for the first round. This will give you greater control over the process flow, and the students will be able to observe the way you turn from one listener to the next, depending on how satisfied you are with the active listening response. Remember to switch back and forth between the role of speaker and that of active listening coach.

Convey It With Feeling
Game and Discussion

Procedure:
Prepare the feeling statements in advance and place them in a container.

Have the students form two teams. Announce that the teams are going to play a game in which members take turns acting out secret statements non verbally. In your own words, explain:

When it is your team's turn, one member will pick a slip of paper from the container and act out the statement for his or her teammates. Try to convey what the statement says through your facial expressions and actions. You may not speak or make noises of any kind. Your teammates will have 1 minute to guess the statement. If they guess correctly, your team will get one point. If they do not guess correctly, the other team will have 30 seconds to try and can also win 1 point. Then it will be the other team's turn to pick a statement from the container and act it out.

Begin the game, keeping time and recording scores on the board. If possible, keep playing until all of the students have had one opportunity to act out a statement.

Objectives:
Group members will:

—convey a variety of feelings nonverbally, and decode them.
—demonstrate and discuss the role of body language in communication.

Materials:
feeling statements written on slips of paper (see below); a small container

Statements:
I feel sad.
I am disgusted.
Leave me alone.
I feel proud.
I am thrilled.
I don't want to do it.
I feel worried.
I don't want anyone to see me.
I am determined.
I am bored to death.

I am furious.
I feel terribly embarrassed.
I am very sorry.
I feel anxious.
I am doubtful.

Conclude the activity with a full-group discussion.

Discussion Questions:

1. Which feelings were hardest to act out? Which were hardest to guess?

2. Why is it useful to be able to understand body language?

3. When someone's word's say one thing and actions say quite a different thing, which do you believe? Why?

4. What feelings do you enjoy showing others? Which ones do you prefer to hide?

5. What have you learned about nonverbal communication from this activity?

The Destroyers
Brainstorming and Role Playing

Objectives:
Group members will:

— brainstorm and list statements that can damage a person's feelings, ideas, and enthusiasm, as well as block communication.
— demonstrate alternative positive statements.
— describe methods of improving communication behaviors in themselves and others.

Materials:
board or chart paper

Procedure:
Facilitate a discussion about appropriate and inappropriate ways to respond to another person's ideas, accomplishments, feelings, etc. In your own words, say:

Have you ever come up with a great idea that you couldn't wait to share with someone? But when you described your idea, the person you told made fun of it, or put you down in some way? Have you been afraid to share your strong feelings about something because you were certain no one would understand or, worse, you'd be ridiculed for your feelings? We can easily destroy a person's enthusiasm just by the things we say. We may not mean to do it, but we can kill their ideas and make them feel foolish for feeling the way they do.

Ask the students to help you brainstorm a list of statements that can hurt communication and damage the feelings, ideas, and enthusiasm of others. Write their ideas on the board or chart paper. Include statements such as:

Can't you see I'm busy?
Not bad for a girl.
Are you kidding me?
You can't be serious!
What a stupid idea!
Just like a guy.
That's a silly question.
You shouldn't feel that way.
Don't be such a wimp.
Who asked for your opinion?

Have pairs of volunteers role play some of the items from the list. Instruct one person to initiate an interaction and the other to respond using the "destroyer" statement. After each role play, ask the actors to describe their thoughts and feelings during the exchange. Then have the group think of at least <u>three alternative positive responses</u> that could be used in that situation. Role play and debrief those as well.

Facilitate a summary discussion.

Discussion Questions:

1. Why do we respond to others with put-downs and other types of destroyer statements?

2. Where do you think we learn this type of communication?

3. If you know someone who frequently makes these kinds of statements to you and others, what can you do about it?

4. How can you change your own bad communication habits?

Extension:

Between sessions, have the group members observe and record all of the destroyer statements they hear at school, home, and play. Discuss their findings at the next session.

I-Messages: Still No Substitute!
Experience Sheet and Discussion

Objectives:
Group members will:

—describe how they typically handle negative feelings in conflict situations.
—practice formulating and delivering I-messages.
—state the benefits of I-messages over other ways of handling negative feelings.

Materials:
one copy of the experience sheet, "I-Messages" for each student; board or chart paper

Procedure:
Ask the students to think of a recent time when they were upset or angry with someone. Give them a few moments to come up with an incident, and then, without using the names of those involved, ask several students to explain:

- the situation
- how they felt
- what they did

As the students describe their experiences, jot down their <u>feelings</u> on the board or chart paper. In addition, list the <u>behaviors</u> they reacted with. For example:

—yelled, fought
—sulked
—threatened
—got even
—silent treatment

Introduce the concept of *I-messages*. In your own words, explain:

Probably the most effective way to deal with negative feelings is to express them honestly and let the other person know what he or she did to cause them. You can do this by using an <u>I-message</u>. An I-message usually begins with the word "I," and has three parts. In the first part you state your feelings ("I feel cheated"); in the second part you describe the behavior that caused your feeling ("...when you eat all the cookies"); and in the third part you explain what you want the person to do ("...and in the future I'd like you to share them with me.").

Communication

Write the formula for constructing an I-message on the board:

I feel _____

when you _____

and I'd like you to _____

I feel _____

because _____

and I want _____

Asked some of the students who shared negative feelings earlier to try formulating an I-message and pretend to say it to the object of their negative feelings (played by you). Coach the students until they demonstrate that they grasp the concept and the formula.

Distribute the experience sheets, and give the students a few minutes to complete them.

Take one situation at a time and ask several students to read their I-messages. Choose one or two I-messages and have volunteers role play them. Debrief each role play, comparing and discussing the effectiveness of the I-messages.

Discussion Questions:

1. As the receiver, how did you feel when you heard the I-message?

2. As the sender, what was it like to state the I-message?

3. Why are I-messages more effective than some of the other ways that we typically handle our negative feelings?

4. When you yell, sulk, call a person names, threaten, or ignore, how much useful information does the other person get about what s/he did or how you would like the situation corrected?

5. What is hardest about using I-messages? What is easiest?

I-Messages
Experience Sheet

Write an I-message for each of these situations. Remember the formula:

I feel... _____ *because/when you...* _____ *and I want...* _____

Your parent tells your brother that he can go to the mall with his friends. When you asked to go to the mall just fifteen minutes ago, the same parent told you "no."

You share a room with your sister. Today was her turn to straighten up and she didn't do it. You are both in danger of being restricted.

Your friend promises to walk home from school with you. You wait and wait, but he/she never shows up. Walking home by yourself, you meet your friend coming down the sidewalk with another kid.

You lend your friend five dollars, which she/he promises to pay back before the end of the week. You need the money for the weekend, but on Friday your friend says she/he doesn't have it.

You tell your best friend a secret that no one else knows. In less than a week, three different kids tell you that they know about your secret. When you ask your best friend about it, he/she shrugs and acts like it's not important.

Communication   Group Activities for Counselors

A Time When It Was Okay to Express My Feelings
A Sharing Circle

Objectives:

Group members will:

—describe incidents in which they were honest about their feelings.
—compare conditions that allow openness with those that do not.

Introduce the Topic:

Our topic today is, "A Time When It Was Okay to Express My Feelings." In this group, we talk about our experiences and how those experiences affect our feelings. In fact, this is a place where we are all encouraged to share our feelings. This is not true of all situations. There are some places where stating one's feelings is neither appropriate nor wise.

Tell us about a time, outside of this group, when it was okay for you to express your feelings. Tell us, too, how you felt experiencing that kind of freedom and acceptance. Maybe something happened at home and your parent made a point of asking how you felt about it. Or maybe there have been times when a friend listened while you really unloaded your feelings. Have you ever expressed your feelings in class, knowing it would be okay?

Think about it for a moment. The topic is, "A Time When It Was Okay to Express My Feelings."

Discussion Questions:

1. How are you affected when our feelings are not accepted?

2. Why do we sometimes keep our feelings to ourselves when we would receive greater acceptance and respect if we expressed them?

3. How can you determine if it's okay to express your feelings?

When Poor Communication Led to Trouble
A Sharing Circle

Objectives:
Group members will:

—describe instances where poor communication led to serious negative results.

—explain how skillful communication prevents interpersonal problems.

Introduce the Topic:
Our topic today is, "When Poor Communication Led to Trouble." Most of us, at one time or another, have been in a situation where people said things they didn't mean, or offended each other with their choice of words, or distorted a message so badly that serious trouble erupted. Has anything like this happened to you? If so, tell us about it.

Maybe you were supposed to pass a message along to someone and didn't get it right, which led to bad feelings between the people involved. Or maybe someone misunderstood what you said and a fight resulted. Have you ever been upset with someone because of his or her tone of voice, or choice of words? Have you ever fumed for days about something a person said, and then realized that the problem was really in the communication, not in the intent? Think about it for a few moments. The topic is, "When Poor Communication Led to Trouble."

Discussion Questions:
1. When you realize that communication has caused a problem, what can you do about it?

2. How does active listening prevent communication problems like these?

3. What other communication skills prevent or help repair misunderstandings?

My Greatest Strength as a Communicator
A Sharing Circle

Objectives:
Group members will:
—identify a communication behavior that they do well.
—describe the benefits of specific communication behaviors.
—explain how communication skills are acquired.

Introduce the Topic:
The topic today is, "My Greatest Strength as a Communicator." Communication takes many forms, and most of us are better in some areas than in others. What do you do best? Maybe you are good at getting the attention of other people. When you say something, everyone listens. Perhaps you have a particularly pleasant voice, or a humorous way of making a point. Or maybe the thing you do best is listen. Do you always seem to understand what people are feeling and trying to say? Other ways of communicating are through writing and artistic expression. Perhaps one of these areas is your strength. Tell us what you do well. Even the smallest thing can be very powerful when people are endeavoring to understand each other. The topic is, "My Greatest Strength as a Communicator."

Discussion Questions:
1. How did you learn the skill or ability you described?
2. How can you use your skill or ability to greatest advantage?
3. Did you hear about some communication skills or traits that you never thought of before? What were they?
4. What abilities did you hear about today that you'd like to develop? How can you acquire them?

PEER RELATIONSHIPS

Getting to Know You
Experience Sheet and Discussion

Objectives:
Group members will:
—describe how a friendship developed.
—identify ways they meet people and make friends.
—state the benefits of enlarging one's repertoire of social skills.

Materials:
one copy of the experience sheet, "Getting to Know You" for each student

Procedure:
Ask the students to think of a friend they currently have, or one they used to have. Invite volunteers to tell the group how they met this person and how the friendship developed. Compare and contrast the various ways in which people can meet.

Distribute the experience sheets and briefly review the directions. Give the students a few minutes to complete the sheet.

If the group is large, have the students share their completed experience sheets in smaller groupings (three to five). If the group is small, complete this portion of the activity as a total group. Lead a culminating discussion. Focus on the benefits of being comfortable with and using many different approaches.

Discussion Questions:
1. Which techniques for making friends are you most comfortable with?
2. Which ways of making friends would you like to become better at?
3. Which ways are you least comfortable with when another person uses them with you?
4. Why is it easy for some people to make friends and harder for others?

Getting to Know You
Experience Sheet

Below are some things that people do to meet and get to know others. Read each item. Check "YES" if it is something you do often. Check "NO" if it is something you almost never do. Check "SOMETIMES" if it is something you do occasionally.

1. Introduce yourself.
This is a great skill to have. Most people are hesitant to walk up to someone they don't know and introduce themselves. So take the lead.
____YES ____ NO ____SOMETIMES

2. Smile.
Sincere smiles are warm and welcoming. They show that you are friendly, and they make other people feel good.
____YES ____ NO ____SOMETIMES

3. Start a conversation.
One of the best ways to start a conversation is to say something about yourself and then ask a question. For example: "I can hardly wait for Spring vacation. My family is going camping. What are you going to do?"
____YES ____ NO ____SOMETIMES

4. Compliment people.
Be generous with praise. When you really like someone's clothes, haircut, drawing or report, say so. Tell a person when you think he or she played a sport or game well.
____YES ____ NO ____SOMETIMES

5. Join organizations; take part in activities.
By joining a club or participating in an activity, you meet people who have interests similar to yours. It's one of the best ways to make friends.
____YES ____ NO ____SOMETIMES

6. Say thank you.
Everyone likes to be appreciated. When someone helps you out, even a little, be sure to show your appreciation.
____YES ____ NO ____SOMETIMES

7. Run for office.
Good leaders are always in demand. Being a leader puts you in the thick of things where you are sure to get to know people.
____YES ____ NO ____SOMETIMES

8. Be a good listener.
Listening to someone shows that you care. Become a good listener and people will seek you out. Why? Because we all like to be listened to, and good listeners are hard to find.
____YES ____ NO ____SOMETIMES

9. Offer to help.
Carry a book, loan a pencil, help solve a problem — notice when people are struggling and offer your assistance. However, always ask first. Sometimes people don't want help.
____YES ____ NO ____SOMETIMES

10. Remember names and use them.
Names are important to people. Using them shows caring and respect.
____YES ____ NO ____SOMETIMES

11. Give parties.
A party doesn't have to be fancy. Just invite some interesting people to get together. Include people you don't know well.
____YES ____ NO ____SOMETIMES

12. Make people laugh.
Laughing feels good. If you can share a funny joke or story once in awhile, people will enjoy being around you. Try not to be a constant clown.
____YES ____ NO ____SOMETIMES

Go back and circle one or two techniques you'd like to learn or use better.

Spinning a Web of Friendships
Art Activity and Discussion

Procedure:
Begin by suggesting an analogy between spider webs and networks of relationships. For example, you might ask the group:

—*How many of you are afraid of spiders?*
—*How do you react when you see a large, intricate spider web?*
—*Have you ever thought of your relationships as a web, with everything and everyone interconnected?*
—*Can you picture each relationship as a strand of the web, delicate in some ways and very strong in others?*

Continue to develop this line of thinking, encouraging the students to point out additional similarities. Then announce that the group is going to create a network of relationship webs, with each person at the center of his or her own web, just like a marvelous, creative spider.

Distribute the art materials. On the board or chart paper, demonstrate by drawing the shapes and patterns of a large spider web. Show how the web begins at the center and expands outward in succeeding tiers. Have the students draw similar webs on their papers. Tell them to write their name in the center of the web and, if they wish, draw themselves as the attendant spider.

On your demonstration web, label a strand emanating from the center with the name of a close friend. Then show how that friend has connected you to other friends and acquaintances by labelling additional strands extending outward from the first and leading toward the outside tiers of the web. Think of another person you know

Objectives:
Group members will:

—compare networks of relationships to intricate spider webs.
—create "relationship webs" demonstrating their own interconnecting relationships.

Materials:
large sheets of drawing paper; colored marking pens; board or chart paper

well and repeat this process. If those two people are connected in any way, show that connection with an intersecting strand.

By now the students will be eager to create their own webs. Circulate and provide reinforcement. Encourage the students to include all sorts of individuals in their webs — not just friends. For example, have them include neighbors, relatives, grocers, hairdressers, bus drivers, and other acquaintances. Even students who perceive themselves as having few friends are connected in various ways to many people in the community. Help them see these interconnections.

When the students have completed their webs, display them on a bulletin board or wall. Give each student an opportunity to explain the intricacies of his/her web to the rest of the group. Don't leave anyone out of this process, even if it means extending the sharing to subsequent sessions.

Facilitate a culminating discussion.

Discussion Questions:

1. What are some ways that our relationship webs interconnect?

2. If each person in our community made a web, would we all interconnect in some way or would some people be isolated? Explain your reasoning.

3. Did anyone's web extend to other countries in the world? Which ones and how?

4. In what ways are relationship strands strong? In what ways are they delicate?

5. Have you ever felt caught in someone else's relationship web and wanted to get out? Tell us what happened, without mentioning names.

Friendship Possibilities
Writing and Sharing Ads

Objectives:
Group members will:
—identify qualities and interests they seek in friends.
—describe their own positive qualities and strengths.
—try new ways of developing friendships.

Materials:
one copy of the experience sheet, "Wanted: A Friend For..." for each student

Procedure:
Begin by asking the students if they have ever seen a "personals" ad. Explain that a personals ad is one in which an individual advertises his/her best qualities in hopes of meeting new friends. Usually, when adults place such ads, they are looking for a romantic relationship. However, sometimes the advertiser simply wants to meet people who share similar interests, like biking, mountain climbing, or dancing.

Announce that the students are going to work in pairs to help each other create friendship ads. Distribute the experience sheets and read through the directions.

Have the students choose partners and assist each other in the creation of ads.

Go around the room and have each person read his/her <u>partner's</u> ad. Ask the group to decide what to do with the ads. Here are some possibilities:

- Attach a snapshot to each ad and create a display in a frequently-used area.
- Submit the ads to the school newspaper.
- Transform the ads into posters and display them around the school.

Discussion Questions:
1. Why do people advertise for friends and companions?
2. What's the difference between stating your positive qualities and bragging?
3. How was this activity helpful to you?
4. How will you respond when people "answer" your ad?

Wanted: A Friend For...
Experience Sheet

Here are two examples of friendship ads. As you can see, they say something about the person advertising, and they describe the qualities and interests desired in a friend.

Nice guy, 14, seeks friends who like video games, roller blading, basketball, computers, and just hanging out. I'm easy going, honest, usually pretty funny, and good in math. I'll help you with algebra if you'll help me mow the lawn, and then we'll share one of my mom's great homemade pizzas.

Athletic girl, 12, looking for an equally athletic friend to run at the lake, join a soccer team or take tennis lessons together. Or maybe become lifeguards? I'm energetic, fun, smart, a loyal friend, and I have a cute older brother. If you can keep up with me, I'll be a great friend.

List the qualities you want in a friend:

_____
_____
_____

List the activities you'd like to share with a friend:

_____
_____
_____
_____

List some of *your* best qualities:

_____
_____
_____
_____

Now write your ad. Make it about 50 words in length. Be clever and creative!

Peer Relationships — Group Activities for Counselors

What's Wrong with This Friendship?
Brainstorming and Situation Analyses

Procedure:
Involve the group in a discussion of some of the main qualities of a good friendship. Solicit qualities from the students and add ideas of your own, listing them on the board or chart paper. Depending on the maturity and sophistication of your group, include some or all of the qualities below; the information in italics is meant to assist you in your elaborations.

Commitment
Being committed to a friendship means being willing to devote time and energy to keeping the friendship alive. It involves communicating, and spending time together sharing interests and activities. Generally speaking, the closer the friendship, the greater the commitment in terms of time and energy.

Acceptance
One of the hallmarks of friendship is the willingness to accept a friend just the way he or she is, complete with feelings, attitudes, beliefs, and behaviors — the ones that annoy you right along with the ones you like.

Objectives:
Group members will:
— identify and describe qualities of a good friendship.
— evaluate the behavior of friends in specific situations.

Materials:
board or chart paper

Trust
Trust between friends develops as they learn to count on each other for support (loyalty), honesty (saying what they mean), and reliability (doing what they say they will do).

Loyalty
Friends do not hesitate to let other people know the value they place on each other and on their relationship. They are steadfast in their willingness to stand up and be counted as a friend.

Dependability

When friends make promises to each other, they keep them. When they plan to do something together, they show up. When they say they will telephone, they do. If a commitment can't be kept for some reason, the other person is notified as soon as possible.

Responsibility/Accountability

Friends don't knowingly do things that hurt or endanger each other. Furthermore, they are accountable for their own actions and don't demand blind loyalty when they do something potentially damaging to themselves.

Slowly read the following situations to the group. After each one, involve the students in a discussion of the situation by asking the questions listed.

Situations:

- Lisa and Debbie have been friends for a long time. They have many of the same interests, even though as people they are very different. Debbie is quiet — maybe even a little shy — while Lisa is outgoing and assertive. These differences never used to cause problems, but lately Lisa has been acting impatient with Debbie. Yesterday, she said that if Debbie doesn't stop acting like such a "wimp," she is going to lose all her friends.

1. *What's wrong with this friendship?*
2. *How would you feel if you were Debbie?*
3. *What do you think will happen?*

- This year, Ken's parents enrolled him in a private school, which means that Ken and his best friend, Bob, no longer see each other every day at school. At first, they made it a point to get together every Saturday and Sunday. Then, after just a few weeks, it was only on Saturdays. Bob would call and ask Ken over, but Ken always seemed to be busy with something else. Now it's getting so Ken and Bob see each other every couple months. When they are together, they don't pal around the way they used to. A lot has changed.

1. *What is missing from this friendship?*
2. *If you were Bob, how would you feel?*
3. *What does it take to keep a friendship going when something like this happens?*

- Hahn and Dennis are neighbors and good friends. They see each other every day. Last week, Hahn confided in Dennis that he really likes Stephanie and would like to ask her to go to the movies. He told no one else. Today, as he is getting ready to leave school, two girls come up to Hahn and start teasing him in front of some other kids. They laugh and sing, "Hahn, we hear you love Stephanie. Have you asked her out yet?" When they see each other later that afternoon, Hahn ignores Dennis.

1. *What's wrong with this friendship?*
2. *If you were Hahn, how would you feel?*
3. *What can Dennis do to repair the damage he's caused?*

- When Veronica, who usually gets average grades, comes out with the highest score on a big math test, someone starts a rumor that she cheated. When a bunch of kids start talking about Veronica at recess, Charlotte says nothing, even though she studied with Veronica and knows how hard Veronica worked to get that grade.

1. *What's missing from this friendship?*
2. *Why didn't Charlotte speak up?*
3. *What would you do in a situation like this?*

- Carol and Liz make plans to meet at the park on Saturday, but Carol never shows up. When Liz calls her, Carol's mom says that Carol went to the shopping mall with some other kids. Liz leaves a message asking Carol to phone her. She never does.

1. *What's wrong with this friendship?*
2. *If you were Liz, how would you feel?*
3. *What do you think Carol should have done?*

- Dale and Maria are looking at videos in a department store. Dale suddenly picks up two videos and puts them in his backpack. Maria protests, but he tells her to hush and act normal. Maria thinks about the situation for a minute, and then tells Dale that she is not going to participate in his stealing. She turns and leaves the store. The next day, Dale yells at Maria and calls her a "lousy friend."

1. *What's wrong with this friendship?*
2. *Do you think Maria handled the situation well? Why or why not?*
3. *Does being loyal to a friend mean that you have to accept everything the person does? Explain.*

Variation:

Duplicate the situations on separate pieces of paper and give them to students to role play for the rest of the group. After each role play, ask the players how they felt in their roles. Then ask the remaining questions and facilitate discussion.

Introduction to Refusal Skills
Presentation, Sharing, and Discussion

Procedure:
Begin by asking the students why they think people — adults and kids alike — so often have difficulty saying no. If the students have trouble answering this question, ask them to think about their own experiences throughout childhood and (for older students) adolescence. Here are some possible reasons:

- Children are taught not to refuse the requests of parents and other authority figures. Sometimes they are punished for refusing.
- Children are taught, instead, to comply with requests, orders, and demands.
- Experience teaches us that saying no frequently causes the other person to feel disappointed, rejected, unhappy, and even angry.
- Most of us learn that it is socially acceptable to conform, do what we're told, and not make waves.
- Most of us — young people especially — want to fit in and be accepted by our peers. We accomplish this by saying yes, not by saying no.

Objectives:
Group members will:

—identify specific reasons why people have trouble saying no.
—describe a situation in which they had difficulty saying no.
—recognize and discuss the goals of refusal skills.

Materials:
board or chart paper

Point out that in the aftermath of all this learning and training, we end up doing things that we don't *want* to do and probably *shouldn't* do. We may even be tempted to do things that we know are *illegal* or *dangerous*. <u>We have to retrain ourselves to say no.</u>

Ask the students to think of a situation in which they had a hard time saying no. Instruct them to write a description of the situation on a slip of paper. Caution them not to use names.

Collect the papers and read some of the situations to the group, discussing each one. Ask the students to explain why the situation was difficult, and what fears are associated with saying no. (**Note:** Save the written situations for the next activity.)

Introduce the concept of *refusal skills*. For example, you might say:

Refusal skills are ways of saying no <u>skillfully</u>. They put you in control of a situation. In the process, you <u>think through</u> the situation and you make a <u>conscious decision</u>.

On the board or chart paper, write the heading ***Goals of Refusal Skills*** and list the following:

- To say no without losing your friends.

- To stay out of trouble.

- To make legal, safe, enjoyable choices.

Conclude the activity by discussing the goals and how refusal skills meet those goals.

Discussion Questions:

1. Why would you want to keep a friend who asks you to do something you shouldn't do?

2. Have you ever succeeded in saying no without making the other person unhappy or angry? How did you do it?

3. How does it feel to stay in control of a difficult situation?

4. How does it feel to get pulled along in a situation you don't want to be part of?

5. Who is in charge of what you say and do?

Using Refusal Skills

Experience Sheet and Role Play

Objectives:
Group members will:

—learn effective methods for saying no.
—practice refusal skills by role playing actual situations.

Materials:
copies of the experience sheet, "The Cool Kid's Guide to Saying No" (recommended for younger students), or "The Smart Student's Guide to Saying No" (for more mature students); the role-play situations saved from the previous activity.

Procedure:
Review the definition and goals of refusal skills (from the previous activity, "Introduction to Refusal Skills").

Distribute the appropriate experience sheet. Read through the refusal skills with the students, answering questions and facilitating discussion.

Read one of the situations saved from the previous activity. Go through the refusal skills, one at a time, explaining how each skill could be used in that situation.

Ask two students to role play the situation in front of the group. Coach the students, as needed.

Read a second situation, only this time ask the <u>students</u> to explain how each refusal skill could be used. Again, ask volunteers to role play the situation. Repeat this process with as many more situations as you have time for. Then lead a culminating discussion.

Discussion Questions:

1. What is the hardest part about using refusal skills?

2. Which steps in the process do you most need to work on?

3. Why is it important to avoid arguing and debating?

4. In what kinds of situations would you want to "keep the door open?" When would this not matter to you at all?

5. What kind of body language is most helpful in situations like these?

6. How can you be sure that you will recall these steps when actually facing a situation?

The Cool Kid's Guide to Saying No

Experience Sheet

What can you say when someone tries to get you to do something you don't want to do? How should you respond when someone asks you to take part in something that is illegal or dangerous?

Say no once. Say no twice. Say no again. Say no and leave. Here are some helpful guidelines:

1. Say no.
Say it clearly, flatly, and confidently. Be assertive. When someone pressures you in a friendly way, remember that you can be friendly too — even humorous — and be assertive at the same time.

2. Say no and give a reason.
Briefly state why you are not going to do whatever the person is suggesting. Use appropriate voice and body language. Let your facial expression show calm confidence. Speak clearly, in a firm, steady voice.

3. Say no and suggest something else to do.
There are lots of ways to have fun. Think of something you both enjoy that is safe and legal. Suggest it, but don't get into a debate.

4. Say no and leave.
Don't waste your time arguing with the person. If steps 1-4 haven't worked, walk away. If you are threatened, skip steps 1-3 and leave immediately.

The Smart Student's Guide to *Saying No*
Experience Sheet

Sometimes people ask you to do things that you're not sure about. Trust your instincts. If you have even the slightest doubt, find out what's really going on. You can gain control of yourself and the situation by following these steps:

1. Get information.
If you have any doubts at all about whether the activity means trouble, ask questions. "Who's going?" "What do you plan to do?" "What will happen then?" "Is it safe?" "Do your parents know about this?" By asking questions, you get everyone to think the situation through. This helps you (and everyone else) gain control.

2. Name the trouble.
As soon as you recognize trouble, put a label on it. "That's stealing." "That's illegal." "That's a lie." Say it clearly and assertively so no one can pretend ignorance.

3. Describe the consequences.
Think about and describe what could happen. Make sure the others understand the risks they are about to take. "You could be arrested." "Your parents will be furious." "That stuff can kill you."

4. Suggest alternatives.
There are many ways to have a good time. Think of something enjoyable that is also safe and legal. "Why don't we all go over to my house instead." "Let's go shoot some baskets." "How about a pizza?"

5. Leave.
If your suggestions don't work, just leave. Arguing and debating are a waste of time and seldom produce results.

6. Keep the door open.
One of the goals of refusal skills is to keep your friends. If that's important to you, try not to judge or condemn anyone. Leave, but leave the door open to future contact. "Okay, *I'm* going to shoot some baskets. Join me later if you change your mind."

When Friends Collide
Sharing Problems and Solutions

Procedure:

Introduce the activity by reminding students of previous activities and discussions about friendship — how to make friends, qualities of a good friendship, etc. Then point out that even the closest friendships sometimes go through rough times. Friendship problems can be caused by conflicts, jealousy, offhanded remarks that lead to hurt feelings, etc.

Ask the students to take out a piece of paper and write down one or two problems they have had recently in their friendships. In your own words explain:

Write down the first couple of problems that come to your mind. These are very likely the ones that bothered (or are bothering) you the most. They don't have to be big issues. Sometimes the smallest things cause the biggest rifts in a relationship.

When the students have finished writing, invite them to share one problem with the group. Caution them not to use the name of the other person involved.

Objectives:
Group members will:

— identify problems they have experienced in friendships.

— suggest and demonstrate possible solutions to friendship problems.

Materials:
chalk board or chart paper

Lead the group in a discussion of each problem shared. Follow these steps in addressing the problem:

1. **Clarify the problem.** Make sure everyone understands what it is in relatively simple terms.

2. **If the problem has more than one part, break it down.** You may want to quickly list these parts on the board or chart paper.

3. **Invite the students to offer ideas for solving the problem** (or a part of the problem). Suggest that the student who shared the problem write down the possible solutions.

4. **Have the student pick one solution to role play.** Have the student take the part of him/herself while volunteers play the friend and any others involved.

5. **Debrief the role play and discuss the effectiveness of the solution.**

Conclude the activity by summarizing and discussing some of the issues that can arise in friendships and the importance of dealing with them. Before closing, remind the students of the confidentiality rule — just in case the identities of friends outside the group became obvious in the course of the activity.

Discussion Questions:

1. What kinds of things seem to cause the most problems in our friendships?

2. Should you try to solve every little problem that arises in a friendship, or is it sometimes better to let things go? Explain.

3. What ideas did you get from this activity about handling friendship problems?

How I Get Attention From the Opposite Sex
A Sharing Cricle

Objectives:
Group members will:
—identify initiating behaviors for attracting the opposite sex.
—explain the role that gaining attention plays in interaction.

Introduce the Topic:
Our topic today is one I think you'll enjoy. It is, "How I Get Attention From the Opposite Sex." When you want to meet a boy or girl, or when you just want someone of the opposite sex to notice you, what do you do? Do you catch the person's eye and smile? Do you flirt, or wave? Or do you just walk up and start talking? Some people get so self-conscious that they begin doing all kinds of awkward or comical things, and it works — they do end up getting attention. Other people recruit a go-between, a friend to deliver a message or arrange an introduction. Still others just start hanging around the person a lot and eventually that person notices. We all have our favorite methods, so tell us about yours. Think about it for a moment or two. Then tell us, "How I Get Attention From the Opposite Sex."

Discussion Questions:
1. What seem to be the most popular ways of getting attention, at least in this group?
2. Why is getting someone's attention an important part of communication?
3. In what ways do the methods we use with the opposite sex differ from the methods we use with the same sex?

A Time I Showed My Feelings for a Friend
A Sharing Cricle

Objectives:
Group members will:

—describe ways in which feelings can be expressed.

—discuss the importance of shared feelings between friends.

Introduce the Topic:
Our topic today is, "A Time I Showed My Feelings for a Friend." Too often, I think, we hide our true feelings from each other. We don't show our friends how much we appreciate, respect, and love them. When our feelings are hurt, we often hide that, too. Expressing feelings can seem risky. But today I want you to think of a time when you took that risk.

Maybe you expressed your feelings in words, or perhaps you showed your feelings in some other way — with a gift or card, a hug, or by doing something special for the person. The feelings you expressed may have been very positive, but they also may have been negative. Showing disappointment, frustration, and sadness can be even more difficult than showing affection. Think about it for a few moments. The topic is, "A Time I Showed My Feelings for a Friend."

Discussion Questions:
1. Why is it difficult to show our feelings?

2. When you showed your feelings, what kind of response did you get from the other person?

3. How does the honest expression of feelings help build trust in a relationship?

A Group I Like Belonging To
A Sharing Cricle

Objectives:
Group members will:

—describe the benefits of belonging to specific groups.

—discuss factors that cause people to associate (or not associate) in groups.

Today our topic is, "A Group I Like Belonging To." One of the most important things in life for most of us is being part of a group of people whom we enjoy and with whom we share common interests or goals. So today we're going to talk about groups we belong to and how it feels to be part of those groups.

If you decide to share, tell us about one group that you consider yourself a part of. The group can be a club or organization here at school, or one that exists outside of school. It can also be a group of friends — students who like each other and hang around together. After you tell us about the group, describe one thing the group does that you enjoy, how you contribute to the group, what the group contributes to you, and how you feel about belonging. Today's topic is, "A Group I Like Belonging To."

Discussion Questions:
1. Why do people join groups, clubs, and organizations?

2. What drew you into the group you described?

3. Why are some people "loners" who rarely associate with groups?

4. How can a group give the impression that it is open to new members?

It Was Hard to Say No, But I Did
A Sharing Cricle

Objectives:
Group members will:
—describe a time when they resisted peer pressure.
—explore effective methods of saying no.

Introduce the Topic:
Today, we're going to talk about times when we were assertive, when we made our own decision and stood up for our wants and needs. Our topic is, "It Was Hard to Say No, But I Did."

Can you think of a time when you said no, even though it was difficult? Maybe a friend tried to talk you into going to a movie instead of finishing your homework and, though tempted, you said no. Maybe someone offered you drugs, and tried to make you feel like a wimp when you refused, but you decided your health was more important than your image and held your ground. Or maybe some friends were trying to get you to drink beer and did everything but pour it down your throat, yet you were able to resist. Have you ever been tempted to cut school, but said no? Have you ever refused someone who offered to trade answers on an exam? Think it over for a minute and then tell us about a time like this in your life. The topic is, "It Was Hard to Say No, But I Did."

Discussion Questions:
1. What were your feelings just before you said no?
2. How do you feel about it now?
3. What methods of saying no work best for you?
4. Why is peer pressure so difficult to resist?

CONFLICT MANAGEMENT

Rules for a Fair Fight
Imagery, Discussion, and Brainstorming

Procedure:
Ask the students to think of a sport or game they enjoy playing—baseball, chess, tennis, volleyball, wrestling, basketball, Monopoly, Scrabble, etc. Tell them to take a few moments, close their eyes, and imagine themselves playing that game with a skilled opponent, being totally involved and energized.

Now, without opening their eyes, ask the students to recall a recent conflict they had with another person—anything from a mild disagreement to a noisy fight. Tell them to picture this contest in as much detail as possible.

Next, suggest that the students allow their minds to transform that image of conflict into a sport or game, seeing it as a contest of opposing ideas, opinions, beliefs, perceptions—whatever it actually was. The opponents in the conflict may not agree, but the fact that they are interacting means that they are playing this game *cooperatively*.

Objectives:
Group members will:

—describe the similarities between a conflict and a game or sport.
—develop rules intended to ensure that conflicts are handled fairly.

Materials:
board or chart paper

Invite the students to open their eyes and comment on this imagery experience. Generate a discussion about the analogy of conflict as game or sport. Encourage the students to further develop the notion, while making key points of your own. For example, you might say:

Conflict is normal. While most of us don't go out the door each morning looking for conflicts, we tend to encounter one or two just about every day. If we think of conflict as a contest — like a tennis match or a game of volleyball — we recognize that it is a cooperative event, a challenge, a test of skills. If we really want to perform well on the conflict court, we have to know the rules of the sport, avoid making too many fouls, present ourselves and our ideas in the most effective ways possible, and respect the rights of our opponent. We have to fight fair. That's why most games have rules. Rules ensure an even start, safety, and adherence to certain agreed-upon behaviors throughout the game. Rules protect both the players and the object of the game.

Ask the students to help you brainstorm some guidelines for "fighting fair." Here are some ideas:

- Identify and focus on the problem.
- Attack the problem, not the person.
- Listen to your opponent.
- Demonstrate respect.
- Take responsibility for your own actions.

Facilitate discussion throughout the brainstorming process.

Discussion Questions:

1. What are some of the benefits of thinking of conflict as a game with rules?

2. When you are in a conflict, how can you encourage the other person to "fight fair."

3. What's wrong with playing by your own set of rules, whether the other person understands them or not?

4. What can you say or do when the other person keeps breaking the rules?

5. What have you learned about conflict from this session?

Extension:

If time permits, brainstorm GAME FOULS. Explain that, just as in a sport, fouls are behaviors that are not allowed because they create an unfair advantage, are disrespectful or dangerous, or destroy the object of the game. Compare the two sets of rules.

First Feelings

Looking at Anger as a Secondary Emotion

Procedure:

Introduce this activity by explaining that anger is a normal emotion, experienced by everyone. However, anger tends to be a *secondary* emotion. In other words, one or more *other* feelings usually come before anger. These can be referred to as "first feelings." Give the students an example, such as: *You forget to study for a test and fail it. Because the test covered a subject in which you usually do well, you feel disappointed and frustrated. However, those "first feelings" quickly turn to anger. Before you know it, anger is the only feeling that you are aware of and the only one other people observe in you.*

Continue by introducing this second and related concept: Other people usually find it hard to deal with our anger. If we become hostile and aggressive when we are angry, we cause others to feel threatened and maybe even to get angry in return. Other people have an easier time responding to our first feeling of disappointment, frustration, embarrassment, grief, or fear.

Objectives:

Group members will:

—identify feelings that typically precede/precipitate anger and identify ways to deal with those feelings.
—practice acceptable ways to express "first feelings."

Materials:

board or chart paper

Consequently, a valuable skill to develop is the skill of identifying and expressing our initial feelings, rather than just our anger. To do this, we need to "buy time" in conflict situations.

Ask the group to think of some initial emotions that often precede anger and write them on the board or chart. They can include feelings such as sadness, grief, frustration, embarrassment, relief, shock, disappointment, and confusion. Then ask the students to suggest acceptable ways of expressing these feelings that others can identify with.

If you need to provide another example of this concept in action, read the following scenario to the group and ask them the questions that follow.

Maria was one of the best players on the hockey team. She really wanted to be captain the coming semester and had more than just a good chance of being elected. Her teammates liked and respected her and she got along well with her coach. Maria knew that her grades had to stay above a C and she struggled to keep her Social Studies grade up. Poor reading skills kept her from doing very well. When she took her final Social Studies test before semester's end, she thought she had done okay. When report cards came out, however, she saw a "D" in Social Studies. During hockey practice after school, Maria announced that she didn't want to be captain of the team. When her friends asked her why she had changed her mind, Maria snapped at them and said, "Who wants to be captain of this stupid team, anyway? I have better things to worry about than keeping you all in line."

—*What were Maria's initial feelings?*

—*How did she express those feelings?*

—*How could Maria have better expressed her emotions?*

Finally, invite group members to describe conflicts that they've experienced recently — preferably ones in which they became angry. Ask them to think back to their very first emotional reaction to the incident and try to pinpoint what it was. This may be difficult for some students, particularly those who have a habit of erupting in anger at the first glimmer of conflict. Keep digging, however. In most cases, other feelings are buried there.

Try role playing the incident. Have the student play him/herself and another member of the group take the role of the other diputant. Employ the <u>alter ego</u> technique, by stationing an additional student next to the central character. Each time this person speaks, allow the alter ego to add comments that express possible thoughts and feelings.

Discussion Questions:

1. How does anger mask what is really going on inside someone?

2. Why is anger so difficult to deal with in other people?

3. Do you think people are sometimes afraid to show their first feelings? Why?

4. What have you learned about your own behaviors from this session?

Exploring Alternatives to Conflict
Dramatizations and Discussion

Objectives:
Group members will:

—learn and practice specific strategies for resolving conflict.

Materials:
one copy of the experience sheet, "Conflict Resolution Strategies," for each student

Procedure:
Distribute the experience sheets. Explain to the students that in conflict situations, certain kinds of behaviors tend to help people solve their problems. As a group, read and discuss the strategies. Give examples, and ask the students to describe problems that might be resolved by each alternative.

Invite a member of the group to describe a conflict situation. Clarify the problem and then engage the group in speculating as to the appropriateness of each strategy in that situation. Ask the group to agree on a strategy to test out. Have members of the group act out the conflict and its resolution, using the alternative chosen. At the conclusion of the role play, debrief the actors and discuss the effectiveness of the solution. Have new actors apply other strategies to the same conflict and discuss those. Then move on to a new conflict situation and repeat the process.

Discussion Questions:
1. Why is it better to practice positive alternatives, rather than wait for a conflict to occur and *then* try them?

2. Which strategies are hardest to use and why? Which are easiest? Which work best and why?

3. At what point do you think you should get help to resolve a conflict?

Conflict Resolution Strategies
Experience Sheet

Have you ever been in a conflict? Of course! No matter how much you try to avoid them, conflicts happen. They are part of life. What makes conflicts upsetting is not knowing how to handle them. If you don't know something helpful to do, you may end up making things worse. So study these strategies, and the next time you see a conflict coming, try one!

1. Share.
Whatever the conflict is over, keep (or use) some of it yourself, and let the other person have or use some.

2. Take turns.
Use or do something for a little while. Then let the other person take a turn.

3. Active Listen.
Let the other person talk while you listen carefully. Really try to understand the person's feelings and ideas.

4. Postpone.
If you or the other person are very angry or tired, put off dealing with the conflict until another time.

5. Use humor.
Look at the situation in a comical way. Don't take it too seriously.

6. Compromise.
Offer to give up part of what you want and ask the other person to do the same.

7. Express regret.
Say that you are sorry about the situation, *without* taking the blame.

8. Problem solve.
Discuss the problem and try to find a solution that is acceptable to both you and the other person.

Problem Solving: The Win-Win Strategy

Experience Sheet and Discussion

Objectives:
Group members will:

—examine a win-win problem solving process and discuss its benefits.
—practice using problem solving to resolve specific conflicts.

Note: This activity works best if it is carried out following the activity, "Exploring Alternatives to Conflict."

Materials:
one copy of the experience sheet, "Getting to Win-Win" for each student; board

Procedure:

Review the strategies for resolving conflict presented in the activity, "Exploring Alternatives to Conflict." Explain that the final strategy — problem solving — is particularly desirable because it promotes positive interaction between disputants, and because both people "win." However, problem solving is also more involved and takes more time.

Distribute copies of the experience sheet and give the students a few minutes to read it. Ask for questions and facilitate a discussion of the benefits of problem solving. For example, you might say:

Of all the strategies for resolving conflicts, problem solving is the most productive—the one most likely to leave both people feeling satisfied. By working together to develop the best possible solution, disputants:

- *interact in positive ways.*
- *listen to each other's concerns.*
- *combine their brain power to create alternative solutions.*
- *choose a solution that allows both to feel they have "won."*

Have the students get together in pairs to practice the win-win process. Tell them to role play a real conflict that one of the partners has experienced recently.

Remind the person with the conflict to describe as accurately as possible both the circumstances of the conflict and the role of the other disputant before starting to role play.

Circulate and monitor the progress of the pairs. Facilitate and provide coaching, as necessary. When most pairs seem to have completed the problem-solving process, lead a discussion.

If time permits, have the students role play a second conflict.

Discussion Questions:

1. How did you feel as you worked together to resolve your conflict?

2. How satisfied are you with your solution? Explain.

3. What are the hardest parts of the process? ...the easiest parts?

4. Problem solving doesn't work for every conflict. When do you think you would use this strategy? For what kinds of conflicts do you think problem solving would be ineffective or inappropriate?

5. What skills do you need to work on in order to improve your ability to handle conflict this way?

Getting to Win-Win
Student Experience Sheet

Have you ever had a conflict with one of your friends? If so, you know how easily conflict can damage a relationship. Sometimes it takes months to patch things up.

Here's a way of handling conflict that can actually make a relationship stronger. By following these steps, you can make sure that both you and your friend end up feeling pretty good. Try it!

When you are in a conflict:

1. Use an I-message to express your feelings and concerns.

2. Try to use a calm tone of voice and open, attentive body language.

3. Listen actively to the other person's side of the story. Don't interrupt. Try to understand his or her perceptions and feelings.

4. If you don't understand something, ask for more information. Say, "Could you tell me more about that..." or "I don't think I understand. What exactly do you mean?"

5. Define the problem. After you have listened to each other's side of the story, work together to agree on exactly what the problem is. Include all parts of the problem in your definition.

6. Brainstorm possible solutions. You might want to write these down. Include all kinds of ideas, even ones that sound a little crazy.

7. Together, agree on the solution that has the best chance of solving the problem (the one you defined together). Combine several alternatives if necessary.

8. If no solution seems possible, put the problem on hold for a few days. Agree on a day and time to get together again. In the meantime, re-think the problem.

Taking Charge of Personal Anger
Small Group Activity and Discussion

Objectives:
Group members will:
- show how a conflict event produces thoughts related to the event, which in turn produce feelings (often anger).
- state that a key to managing anger is buying time to think.
- practice substituting moderate thoughts for angry thoughts as one way of reducing anger.

Materials:
board or chart paper

Procedure:
Explain that the group is going to demonstrate how buying time will allow them the opportunity to change their thoughts about conflict situations which in turn can reduce anger.

Write four headings across the top of the board or chart: **Event, Thoughts, Feelings,** and **Substitute Thoughts.** Under the **Event** column write *Mom won't let me go to the dance with my friends.* Skip the second column and ask the students what their feelings might be in this situation. The students will probably suggest words such as mad, furious, and miserable. Write several of these words in the **Feelings** column. Then go back to the **Thoughts** column, and ask the students what their thoughts might be concerning the same situation. Elicit answers such as these: *She's being mean or unreasonable. She doesn't understand how important it is to me. She never wants me to have fun.*

Explain to the students that it is not the event, but the *thoughts* about the event that cause the feelings. Refer to the sentences in the second column and point out that any of these thoughts about the event could create angry feelings. Explain that no situation, event, or person *makes* us have a particular feeling. Through our thoughts, we *choose* our feelings, even if we are not aware of it.

Next, suggest that if the thoughts recorded in the second column can be moderated, the feelings too will change. Help the students create new thought statements such as: *Mom thinks she is looking out for my safety. She has family plans the night of the dance and wants me to be with the family. There will be more dances this year.* Record them in the last column, **Substitute Thoughts**. Point out that these moderated thoughts will reduce the anger.

Ask the students to divide a sheet of paper in half lengthwise creating two columns. Have them write the heading *Event* at the top of the left-hand column and the heading *Thoughts* at the top of the right-hand column. Next, instruct the students to turn their paper over and create two more columns. Direct them to write the headings *Feelings* and *Substitute Thoughts* above the left and right columns on this side.

Under the first heading, ask the students to list three real or hypothetical situations/events in which they are certain they would feel angry. In the second column (adjacent to each description), have them write the thoughts they would have in each situation. On the other side of the paper, ask them to write down the feelings that these thoughts would create. Finally, challenge the students to come up with different thoughts that could be substituted for the original thoughts.

When all of the students have completed their charts, invite individuals to share their analysis of one conflict. After each example, ask the group how their feelings might change as a result of the substitute thoughts. Emphasize that when they find themselves reacting to a situation too strongly, they can improve the situation and their disposition by rethinking the situation. To do this, they need to buy time. Both abilities take practice and perseverance, but they work!

Discussion Questions:

1. Why do we choose to feel angry in certain situations?

2. When you are angry, why is it important to "buy yourself some time" to rethink the situation?

3. What's the hardest thing about changing your thoughts in a situation?

4. What have you learned about your own anger from this session?

Criticism — Just Handle It!
Dyads and Discussion

Objectives:
Group members will:
—describe a recent criticism they received.
—explain why criticism is often perceived as threatening.
—examine and discuss a four-step process for dealing effectively with criticism.

Materials:
board and chalk

Procedure:
Before the session, write the following discussion topic on the board:

"A Recent Criticism I Received"

Announce that the group is going to examine a type of communication that people give each other all the time, even though practically no one likes to receive it. Quite often this type of communication leads to conflict. Announce that the subject of the session is *criticism*.

Have the students choose partners and move their desks or chairs together so they can talk quietly. Then, draw their attention to the topic on the board. Direct the partners to take 1-2 minutes each to speak to this topic. When it is their turn to listen, they should do so attentively, without interrupting. When it is their turn to speak, they should describe the criticism they received, the "first feelings" they experienced upon hearing it, and how they responded. Reassure the students that it doesn't matter whether the criticism was true or untrue. The validity of the criticism should not be the focus of sharing.

When the dyads are finished, generate a full group discussion using these questions:

—*How did you respond to the criticism you described?*

—*If the criticism led to a conflict, how could the conflict have been avoided?*

Next, write the following guidelines on the board:

STEPS IN HANDLING CRITICISM

1. BUY YOURSELF SOME TIME!!!!!

2. If the criticism is true, agree.

3. If you are unsure, ask for specifics and clarification.

4. If it is not true, state and reaffirm your position, or simply ignore the criticism.

Go over the steps with the group, inviting student input and examples, and elaborating on each point. Facilitate discussion, making as many of these points as possible:

- Some people handle criticism well, but most are threatened by it to some degree.

- The brain reacts to any perceived threat by releasing chemicals into the blood stream. Buying time (the first rule of conflict management) gives these chemicals a chance to dissipate so that negative feelings can begin to go away.

- Use active listening to consciously hear and consider a criticism. If the criticism is valid, say so. *You may want to thank the person.*

- If you don't understand the criticism, ask questions to get more information and clarification.

- If you decide that the criticism is *not* true, either 1) restate your position with an I-message and answer any questions the other person may have, or 2) thank the person for sharing and forget the whole thing.

Discussion Questions:

1. What is the most common reaction or "first feeling" we have after receiving criticism and why do we feel it? (defensiveness—because we are threatened)

2. What role does buying time play in turning the receipt of criticism into a positive experience?

3. What can happen if we don't manage criticism well?

4. What did you learn from this session?

Extension:

Have the students practice the four-step process by role playing the situations they shared in their dyads. Conduct at least two demonstration role plays in front of the group, utilizing volunteers. Provide appropriate coaching and reinforcement. Then allow the students to return to their dyads for practice.

Managing Moods

Experience Sheet and Discussion

Objectives:

Group members will:

—explain how moods are affected by feelings left over from conflicts.
—identify problems and feelings associated with specific conflicts.
—describe strategies for releasing residual feelings and managing negative moods.

Materials:

one copy of the experience sheet, "Three Lousy Moods," for each student; board or chart paper; 3" x 5" index cards

Procedure:

Begin by asking the group: *Have you ever been in an extremely bad mood because of something negative that happened in one relatively small area of your life?*

Invite volunteers to briefly share their "bad mood" experiences. Then, ask for a show of hands from students who have behaved badly toward a friend or family member for no particular reason other than they were in a bad mood. Point out that this sort of thing happens all the time.

Distribute the experience sheets and quickly go over the directions. Allow the students to work two's or three's to complete the sheet. Allow about 10 minutes.

Take a few minutes to discuss the three scenarios described on the experience sheet. Looking at one scenario at a time, ask the students how they answered the questions. Help the students recognize and describe how Ahmad, Rita, and Mike each started with a specific problem or conflict which produced certain feelings (frustration, worry, disappointment, anxiety, embarrassment, etc.). In all three cases, these first feelings were followed by anger, and the anger carried over into unrelated activities involving unsuspecting friends.

Write the following guidelines on the board:

> **GUIDE TO MANAGING MOODS**
>
> 1. BUY YOURSELF SOME TIME!!!!!
> 2. Fill this time with mood management strategies.
> 3. It takes time for feelings to go away naturally. Don't let them affect other activities.

Ask the students: *Why is it so important to "buy time" when you are experiencing negative feelings associated with a problem or conflict?*

Facilitate a discussion around the three guidelines, inviting input and examples from the students, and making these points:

- The feelings we take away from a conflict (residual feelings) tend to stay with us for some time. Even a well-managed conflict is stressful, and left over feelings carry over into other activities and relationships. In addition, they can be hard on us physically.

- Internal conflicts, or conflicts that cannot be immediately resolved for one reason or another, also produce stress. Negative feelings may be with us constantly until the problem is resolved.

- Residual feelings and feelings associated with unresolved conflict affect our moods.

- The use of *mood-management strategies* can help us relieve stress and negative feelings, lessening the chance that a "bad mood" will result in damage to our body, our relationships, and other areas of our life.

On the board, write the heading, "**Mood Management Strategies**." Ask the students to help you brainstorm positive, healthy ways of releasing anger and other negative feelings. List all ideas. Include items such as:

- Talk with a trusted friend or adult.
- Run laps around the block or track.
- Leave the situation and take several slow, deep breaths.
- Get something to eat or drink.
- Listen to relaxing music.
- Take a walk in a pleasant natural setting.
- Imagine being in a favorite place.
- Work on a project or hobby.

Give each student a 3" x 5" card. Suggest that the students write down three or four mood management ideas that they think might work for them. Encourage them to carry the card with them, or tape it to a mirror or closet door at home as a reminder.

In subsequent sessions, ask volunteers to report on their progress using mood management strategies. Frequently remind the students that these strategies are short-term controls, not permanent solutions to big problems. However, they do relieve stress and allow us to enter into problem solving and conflict resolution with greater self-control and productivity.

Three Lousy Moods

Student Experience Sheet

Read the following scenarios. Write your answers to the questions on the other side of the sheet.

Scenario 1:
Ahmad was just finishing a report on the computer when he hit the wrong key and erased all of his work. He felt totally frustrated and starting to get angry with himself, but he had to get to his next class. Ahmad walked out of the computer room and down the hall. Lost in his thoughts about doing something so stupid, he stumbled right into Judy, knocking her books all over the floor. Then he gave her a disgusted look and yelled, "Why don't you look where you're going."

Questions:
—What was Ahmad's real problem?
—What were his first feelings about that problem?
—What were some of his other feelings?
—What did Judy do that caused Ahmad to behave toward her the way he did?
—Why did Ahmad yell at Judy?

Scenario 2:
Rita was ready to leave for school, but she couldn't find her books and nobody seemed to know where they were. She had two assignments due that day and both were inside her books. She started to get upset. After nearly thirty minutes of searching, Rita found the books in one of her little sister, Martha's, favorite hiding places. When she confronted her, Martha admitted hiding them. Even though she found her books, Rita was still mad at her sister and left for school late and in a terrible mood. When she walked into her first class, her best friend Cathy said, "Hi girl, you look upset." Rita snapped, "Leave me alone, I don't want to talk to you!"

Questions:
—What was Rita's real problem?
—What were her first feelings about that problem?
—What were some of her other feelings?
—What did Cathy do that caused Rita to respond the way she did?
—Why did Rita snap at Cathy?

Scenario 3:
Mike just found out that he didn't make the final cut for the basketball team. As he walked away from the gym, he started feeling angry. Mike thought it was unfair that some of the guys who did make the team couldn't shoot or maneuver nearly as well as he could. He felt crummy. When he walked around the corner, Mike saw a bunch of his friends talking. When Charlie saw Mike, he said, "What are you looking so down about?" Mike was embarrassed. He didn't want anyone to know he'd been cut, so all he said was, "None of your business," and walked off.

Questions:
—What was Mike's real problem?
—What were his first feelings about that problem?
—What were some of his other feelings?
—What did Charlie do that caused Mike to behave the way he did?
—Why was Mike rude to his friends, and why did he just walk off?

I Got Into a Conflict
A Sharing Cricle

Objectives:
Group members will:
—describe conflicts they have experienced and what caused them.
—describe ways of dealing with the feelings of others in conflict situations.
—identify strategies for resolving conflicts with peers and adults.

Introduce the Topic:
Our topic today is, "I Got Into a Conflict." Conflicts are very common. They occur because of big and little things that happen in our lives. And sometimes the littlest things that happen can lead to the biggest conflicts. This is your opportunity to talk about a time when you had an argument or fight with someone. Maybe you and a friend argued over something that one of you said that the other didn't like. Or maybe you argued with a brother or sister over what TV show to watch, or who should do a particular chore around the house. Have you ever had a fight because someone broke a promise or couldn't keep a secret? If you feel comfortable telling us what happened, we'd like to hear it. Describe what the other person did and said, and what you did and said. Tell us how you felt and how the other person seemed to feel. Take a few moments to think about it. The topic is, "I Got Into a Conflict."

Discussion Questions:
1. How did most of us feel when we were part of a conflict?
2. What kinds of things led to the conflicts that we shared?
3. How could your conflict have been prevented?
4. What conflict management strategies could have been used in the situations that we shared?

A Time I Was Afraid to Face a Conflict
A Sharing Cricle

Objectives:

Group members will:

—explain how fear can inhibit effective conflict management.
—identify skills for resolving conflict.

Introduce the Topic:

Our topic today is, "A Time I Was Afraid to Face a Conflict." Have you ever been in a dispute with someone that was sort of "underground?" In other words, there was some kind of misunderstanding, or a build-up of negative feelings, but you didn't want to confront them?

Maybe the other person said something to you that really upset you, but you were afraid to talk to him or her about it. Perhaps the person didn't keep a promise or a commitment of some kind, and you were very disappointed, but didn't want to make a big issue of it. Or maybe you could tell that someone was angry with you, so you avoided the person because you didn't want to fight. Think about it for a few moments. When you take your turn, tell us what happened and what you were afraid would occur if you confronted the problem. Our topic is, "A Time I Was Afraid to Face a Conflict."

Discussion Questions:

1. What were most of us afraid would happen if we faced our conflict?

2. If you ignore a conflict, how likely is it to go away by itself? Explain your reasoning.

3. What skills can help you face and handle conflict more easily? What attitudes help?

A Time We Needed Help to Resolve a Conflict
A Sharing Cricle

Objectives:
Group members will:
—describe a conflict in which the help of a third party was needed.
—identify helpful behaviors on the part of a conflict mediator.

Introduce the Topic:
Our topic for this session is, "A Time We Needed Help to Resolve a Conflict." All of us get into conflicts with our family and friends. Much of the time, we work things out without getting anyone else involved. But sometimes a conflict is too big or too upsetting to handle without help. Can you remember such a time? Maybe you and a brother or sister were arguing over whose turn it was to mow the lawn, and you had to ask one of your parents to help figure it out. Or maybe you had a conflict with a friend over something you were told he or she said about you behind your back, and it took the help of another friend to get the two of you back together. Perhaps you and a classmate had to ask the teacher to settle an argument over who had the correct answer to a problem, or maybe you had to let your coach help settle a fight between you and a teammate. Think about it for a few moments, and tell us what the conflict was about and what the third person did to help you settle it. The topic is, "A Time We Needed Help to Resolve a Conflict."

Discussion Questions:
1. What were some of the reasons that we had to ask for help?
2. When is it a good idea to let someone else help you resolve a conflict?
3. If you ask for help resolving a conflict and the person you ask just comes over and tells you what to do, is that helpful? Why or why not?
4. What kind of help is helpful in resolving a conflict?

SUCCEEDING IN SCHOOL

Conflict Management — Group Activities for Counselors

Actions and Consequences
Situations and Discussion

Procedure:
Tell the students that you are going to read aloud a situation involving a student. Read one of the scenarios on the opposite page. Then, one at a time, ask the group these questions, facilitating discussion between questions:

—What was the student's <u>behavior</u>?
—What were the <u>consequences</u> of the student's behavior?

Use the first example to define the words *behavior* and *consequences*. When you are satisfied that the students understand both terms and their relationship to each other, read aloud the remainder of the situations, discussing each one. Ask the students to answer this additional question:

—Did the student have any <u>control</u> over the consequences? If so, what? If not, why not?

From the hypothetical situations, move to real ones. Ask volunteers to describe their own recent behaviors (preferably having to do with school) and the consequences that followed. Again, discuss the degree to which the student was able to control the consequences.

Objectives:
Group members will:

—define the terms behavior and consequences.
—identify possible consequences of specific behaviors.
—explain how consequences can be controlled in some situations.

Materials:
none

Additional Discussion Questions:
1. Who was in control of the person's behavior in most of these situations?

2. What are some behaviors that have no consequences at all?

3. If you desire certain consequences, how can you choose behaviors that you know will result in those consequences? Explain.

Situations:

Linda is daydreaming in class. When the teacher calls on her, she has no idea why. She didn't even hear the question, so she certainly doesn't know the answer.

Ruben's friends ask him to join in a basketball game after school. Ruben remembers that he has a project due the next day and explains that he doesn't have time to play.

Barb and Sue have an argument on the way to school. They are still trying to resolve their disagreement when the bell rings. By the time the matter is settled, they are several minutes late to class.

Richard sets his backpack on the front lawn of the school while waiting for his ride. He wanders away to talk with friends. When he returns, the pack is gone. In addition to his books, Richard loses a report that he's been working on for two weeks. It's due tomorrow, and he won't make it.

Some girls are sharing a cigarette in the bathroom when Dana enters. They ask Dana to join them. She says no and starts to leave. The girls call her chicken, and one of them verbally threatens her.

The teacher tells the class to take notes while she goes over a complicated problem in math. John always gets A's in math, so he doesn't bother. When the same problem shows up on the next day's quiz, John can't remember how to solve it.

Extension:

Distinguish between *natural* and *logical* consequences. For example, a natural consequence of getting into a fist fight is physical injury. A logical consequence, if the fight occurs on the school grounds, is receiving a referral to the principal.

Input, Output

Discussion and Ongoing Self-Assessment

Objectives:

Group members will:

—describe the relationship between input and output generally, and between effort and results in school.

—assess their efforts on multiple school assignments.

Materials:

board or chart paper; 2-cup measuring cup; container of water

Procedure:

Write this familiar adage on the board for the students to see when they arrive for group:

You get out of life what you put into it.

Ask the students what this statement means to them. Many students will have heard it before, but most will have given it little thought; some will find it tired and boring. However, see what kind of discussion you can spark.

Draw a line between the words *life* and *what*, and label the two parts of the statement **Output** and **Input**. Beneath the first statement, add these related statements:

You get out of school / as much as you put into it.

You get out of a project / as much as you put into it.

Ask the students to brainstorm some examples of what **Input** and **Output** might consist of relative to a class project, test, or homework assignment. Depending on the specificity with which the students approach this question, you could end up with two quite long lists. However, in general terms, these are the kinds of examples you are after:

Input	Output
effort	learning
time	satisfaction
interest	recognition
enthusiasm	grade

Ask the students to think of times when they proved this adage by getting out of an assignment just about exactly what they put into it. Encourage them to see the relationship between little effort, time, interest, etc., and little learning plus a low grade, as well as the relationship between much effort and a high grade.

Produce the measuring cup and container of water, and ask a student to pour about 1/4 cup of water into the measuring cup. Then ask the entire group:

— *How much water went into the measuring cup?*
— *What's the most water you can get out of the measuring cup?*
— *If you tried all day, could you get 1/2 cup of water out of the measuring cup? Why not?*

(This may seem awfully simple, but it makes a point.)

Ask the students to take out a sheet of paper and draw a small measuring cup in the upper right-hand corner. Tell them to draw lines on the cup to represent the quantity markers. Draw an example on the board or chart.

Tell the students that on every paper, homework assignment, and test they turn in to a teacher during the remainder of the group's time together, you want them to draw a small measuring cup, and fill it in showing how much effort they put into that assignment. On your example measuring cup, fill in the space up to the 1/4 cup line. Then, in your own words, make these points:

I am not asking you to put any more effort into your assignments than you would otherwise choose to do. I am asking you to be aware of the effort you put in and compare it to the results you get back. As soon as your work is returned to you, please bring it to group so that we can discuss your personal observations about the relationship between input and output.

At each succeeding session, remind the students to continue using this technique, and take a few minutes to discuss the results that students have brought in.

Discussion Questions:

1. How did you feel when you drew and filled in the measuring cup? What were your thoughts?

2. On what did you base your input rating? Do you think you were fair?

3. How closely did your input and output match? Did you get the grade you expected based on your effort?

4. Has this technique had any effect on the way you do your schoolwork? What has changed?

Effectively Managing Time
Experience Sheet

Procedure:
In your own words, say to the group:

By following a few simple rules and acquiring good time management habits, you can accomplish more and have more time for yourself, too. Time management helps you get things done on time so you can avoid last minute rush jobs and the feeling of being unprepared. By planning your activities at school, home, and work, you'll get the most out of each day and you won't feel like you've wasted the time you do have.

Ask the students to form four groups. Assign each group one of the strategies listed below. Tell the groups that you would like them to brainstorm all the ideas and specific behaviors they can think of that might fit within that category.

Objectives:
Group members will:

—keep track of their time use for one week.
—identify specific ways of organizing their time and surroundings.

Materials:
chart paper and a marking pen for each group; masking tape; one copy of the experience sheets, "Keeping a Time Log" and "Time Management Tips for each student

Time Management Strategies:
1. Organize Your Time
2. Prioritize Your Activities
3. Organize your home environment
4. Organize your school environment

Ask the group with Strategy 1 to post its list. Discuss the suggestions that the students have come up with. Liberally underline, star, and number selected strategies to prioritize and reinforce them. Follow the same procedure for each of the other strategies. Below are some key behaviors to add if the students have not thought of them.

Strategy 1:

Organize Your Time

—Keep a planning calendar.
—Record all the things you must do.
—Check your calendar first thing every morning.

Strategy 2:

Prioritize Your Activities

—Decide what's most important, second most important, and so on.
—Do the most important things first.

Strategy 3:

Organize your home environment

—Have a place to study and a surface (or computer) to write on.
—Reduce or eliminate distractions.
—Keep materials and equipment handy.

Strategy 4:

Organize your school environment

—Keep an orderly locker, backpack, and notebook.
—Hold a clean-up, throw-out and get-organized session each night.
—Make sure you have all supplies and assignments ready for the next day.

Distribute the experience sheets. Explain to the students that keeping a time log for a few days will help them recognize where they need to make changes in their use of time. Go over the codes and directions. Review and discuss the "Time Management Tips" on the second page of the experience sheet. If you are meeting with the group weekly, ask them to bring their completed time logs to the next session.

At a follow-up session, invite the students to share highlights from their time logs. Discuss how they can use this information, along with the Time Management Strategies, and the "Time Management Tips" to gain better control of their activities and responsibilities.

Discussion Questions:

1. How satisfied are you with your use of time?

2. Where do you most need to get organized?

3. How do you usually waste time?

4. How can you reduce or eliminate wasted time?

5. Why is it important to find time for work and relaxation?

6. How much time do you spend watching TV? Do you have any desire to change that figure? Why or why not?

7. What have you learned from these activities?

Keeping a Time Log
Experience Sheet

Directions: Keep track of your time for one week. Every day, in each square of the log, write the code that stands for the activity you did during that time period. Make up your own codes for activities that are not listed.

CODES:
- **CL**: Class time
- **FM**: Family activity
- **HO**: Hobby
- **ET**: Eating
- **FR**: Time with friends
- **ST**: Studying
- **SH**: Shopping
- **SL**: Sleeping
- **SP**: Sports
- **TE**: Telephone
- **TV**: Television
- **TR**: Traveling to and from...
- **CH**: Chores
- **RE**: Relaxing

	Monday	Tuesday	Wednesday	Thursday	Friday	Saturday	Sunday
6 am							
7 am							
8 am							
9 am							
10 am							
11 am							
12 pm							
1 pm							
2 pm							
3 pm							
4 pm							
5 pm							
6 pm							
7 pm							
8 pm							
9 pm							
10 pm							
11 pm							

Time Management Tips

1. **Learn to say "no."** If someone wants you to do something that you aren't interested in doing, its okay to turn down the offer. In the same way, assert your rights when someone is wasting *your* time. You have the right to make good use of your time and energy. Do things that you really enjoy and benefit from. Spend time with people who add to your life.

2. **Make decisions.** Low energy and confusion sometimes result from failing to act when decisions need to be made. By making decisions and following through, you spend your time on important tasks instead of wasting it on worry or confusion.

3. **Look ahead and set goals.** Everyone should have short-term and long-range goals. You can set goals as far ahead as you choose. Stay flexible but start preparing now for the future.

4. **Get your body and mind in shape.** Budget some time for exercise and make sure you eat right and get enough sleep. When you feel rushed or stressed during the day, take a break and relax.

5. **Tackle the toughest part of any job or assignment first.** Don't start with the easy stuff. Take advantage of your freshness and enthusiasm when you first begin work. Accomplishing the tough part will spur you on to complete the rest of the task.

6. **Don't put things off.** Procrastination is the biggest obstacle between you and increased effectiveness. Start now and take each project one step at a time. Keep moving and strive to eliminate procrastination from your life.

7. **Be flexible.** Things are always changing. Be willing to adapt and switch directions if new circumstances or information arise. Be open to new possibilities.

Improving Study Skills
Experience Sheet and Discussion

Objectives:
Group members will:
—learn and practice effective study habits.
—develop and implement plans for self-improvement.

Materials:
one copy of the experience sheet, "Study Skills Assessment" for each student; board or chart paper

Procedure:
Begin by asking the students where and how they study. Call on volunteers to share their study strategies. List particularly helpful or innovative ideas on the board or chart paper.

Distribute the experience sheets and give the students a few minutes to complete them. Then discuss each item. Ask the students how they interpreted and answered the questions, and give them additional pointers from the information below. While you write key words and phrases on the board or chart paper, suggest that the students record notes directly on the experience sheet.

Study Skills and Habits

1. **Know your learning style.** Where and how do you study best? Do you like to work alone, with a friend, at the library, or at a desk in your room? Do you learn best by outlining, making mind maps, drawing diagrams, reading, acting things out, or talking over ideas with someone?

2. **Study the difficult subjects first.** The harder assignments take more energy than the easier ones, so save the "light" things for later.

3. **Take short, frequent breaks during study sessions.** Whenever possible, study for approximately 20 minutes and take a 5-minute break. You'll tend to remember better what you learn at the beginning and end of each study period, so create more beginnings and endings. Give your brain a break.

4. **Set goals for your study time.** Decide ahead of time how far you plan to read, how many questions you will answer, or how many problems you will solve. Then stick to your goals.

5. **Have a special study area.** Most students study best in a quiet place, away from the phone and TV. Using a desk or table is better than lying across your bed. Give your body the signal that it is time to study, not time to sleep.

6. **Study effectively.** Look at headings and subheadings. Answer questions and read summaries at the end of chapters. Write down important terms and vocabulary, as well as any questions you have. See how much information you can get from looking at graphs and diagrams. Read new information more slowly. Skim to review.

7. **Study regularly.** Don't save everything until the last minute. Study often enough and for long enough periods to get your work done without "cramming." Cramming is stressful — physically and mentally.

8. **Pretend you are a "paid" student.** If you were employed as a student, would you be earning your wages? If your breaks were longer than your study sessions, you would probably have your pay "docked," or lose your job.

Ask the students to choose at least one skill or strategy and commit to trying it over the weeks that the group meets. Lead a culminating discussion.

Discussion Questions:

1. What is meant by *learning style*?

2. Why is it important to study in ways that are in keeping with your learning style? What happens if you don't?

3. How can you improve your study habits?

4. Which study tips do you plan to try?

5. Whom do you need to ask for help or support in order to carry out your improved study plan?

Study Skills Assessment
Experience Sheet

Answer these questions about your study habits. Read each question and mark the answer that best describes you at this time.

1. Do you know and use your best learning style?

    Always / Sometimes / Seldom / Never

2. Do you study the difficult subjects first?

    Always / Sometimes / Seldom / Never

3. Do you take short, frequent breaks during study sessions?

    Always / Sometimes / Seldom / Never

4. Do you set goals for your study time?

    Always / Sometimes / Seldom / Never

5. Do you have a special study area?

    Always / Sometimes / Seldom / Never

6. Do you read and study effectively?

    Always / Sometimes / Seldom / Never

7. Do you study regularly?

    Always / Sometimes / Seldom / Never

8. If you were a "paid" student, would you earn your wages?

    Always / Sometimes / Seldom / Never

Mind-Mapping
Experiment and Discussion

Procedure:
Begin by asking if the students enjoy looking at and reading maps. Ask the students who answer affirmatively to describe what they like about maps. Their answers are likely to suggest that they:

—enjoy finding their way around using a map.
—like the appearance of the shapes, grids, symbols, etc.
—appreciate the geographical information maps give.
—are good at assimilating and interpreting spatial information.

Tell the students that there is a very effective and fun way to take notes called mind-mapping that will allow them to turn almost any kind of information into a map, and:

—find their way around the subject.

—use various line configurations and symbols to show meaning and relationships.

—create a "geographical" representation of the subject.

Objectives:
Group members will:

—learn a graphic style of note-taking.
—construct at least two practice mind maps.

Materials:
chart paper and colored markers; a newspaper, magazine, or book

In your own words, elaborate:

A mind-map is pretty much what its name implies. It's a map or chart that you construct as you listen to your teacher or as you read a chapter in your book. Each time you put down a new piece of information, its relationship to previously recorded information is shown by where you place it. The main subject is usually pictured or symbolized in the center of the page, and the major ideas are shown as branches emanating from that central point. Examples, details, and questions emanate from the main branches. A mind-map has an organic tree-like look. It can continue to grow in any or all directions as you gather more facts and information, think of questions, and see new relationships. There is no right or wrong way, no correct or incorrect order for making a mind-map. In fact, the more relaxed and creative you are in making a mind map, the more closely the map will resemble the way the same information has been organized inside your brain!

Give the newspaper, magazine, or book to a student, and ask him/her to read any article or chapter, beginning with the title. As the student reads, create a mind map of the information. Allow the reading to continue until you have been able to construct a map with several levels of branching information. Use different colored markers and, if possible, include symbols as well as words.

Once you have modeled the process, give the students a chance to try mind-mapping. Have them take out paper and pencils and create a mind map from information you read to them. (Preselect this passage to ensure that it is easy to follow and conducive to mapping.)

Have the students show each other their mind maps. Answer any questions, and then repeat the process using a different passage. Emphasize that mind-mapping is a highly personal exercise, and that everyone's style of mapping is a correct style.

Encourage the students to use mind-mapping as a way of outlining chapters in books, planning projects, and taking notes in class.

Discussion Questions:

1. What do you like best about mind-mapping? What are you having trouble with?

2. How does mind-mapping compare with outlining?

3. In which subjects do you think mind-mapping will be most useful? Why?

4. What kinds of decisions did you have to make as you created your maps?

5. Do you think a mind map is ever finished? Why or why not?

If you wish to learn more about mind mapping, an excellent resource is: *Mapping Inner Space* by Nancy Margulies,

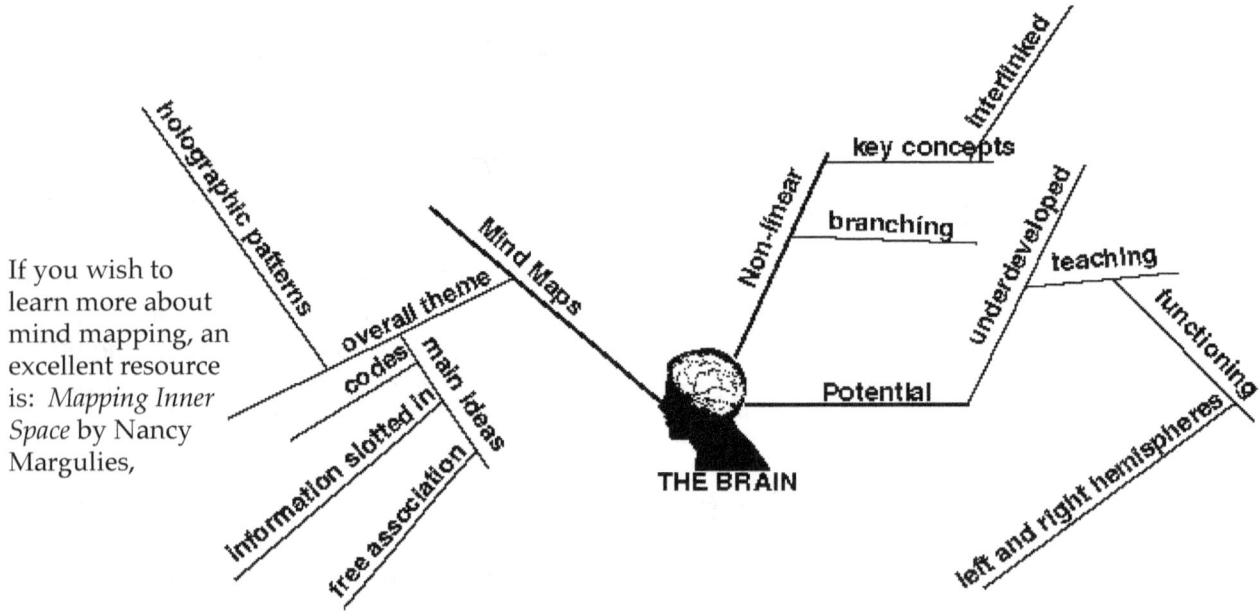

Setting and Attaining Goals
Discussion and Experience Sheet

Objectives:
Group members will:

—explain that having a goal is the first step to achieving what one wants.
—identify specific steps for attaining goals.
—develop skills in setting practical and achievable goals.
—experience goal attainment.

Materials:
pens or pencils, blank note paper, the experience sheets, "You Can Reach Your Goals!" and "Tips for Setting Goals" (one copy for each student)

Procedure:
This is a continuing activity, designed to be used with students over several weeks. It will allow them to experience the satisfaction of setting and achieving goals that are important to them, and will teach them an effective goal-setting process.

Introduce the activity. Explain to the students that most successful people have a habit of setting clear goals concerning things that they want to accomplish. Explain that in this activity, the students will set goals and experience the feeling of success that comes with attaining them.

Point out that when we think of goals, we usually picture big, important things like cars, houses, vacations, etc., but that we set dozens of smaller goals each day. Ask volunteers to share some of the things they want to accomplish today. Point out that stating these things is the simplest form of goal setting.

Distribute both experience sheets. Review PART 1 of the goal-setting experience sheet, offering an example or two to illustrate each point. Then give the students a few minutes to complete the first part of the sheet, writing down their goals and answering the questions.

If possible, spend a few moments with each student, reviewing his or her goals to make sure that they are attainable, properly written, and within the purview of the student to achieve (not dependent on events or people outside the student's control).

Explain that goals are achieved in steps. Success is measured as each step is completed. Point out that PART 2 of the experience sheet helps the students break down their goals into more easily managed steps.

Allow 10 to 15 minutes for the students to write down the steps for each goal. While they are writing, offer assistance. This task will be foreign to most students and they will need guidance in formulating the steps. Again, you can add significantly to this activity by sitting with each student and assisting in the development of the steps — particularly for those goals that pertain to school achievement.

Direct the students to keep their experience sheets and refer to them daily as they work toward their goals. Review the progress of the students regularly in group. Lead a discussion after each review.

Discussion Questions:

1. How do you feel about having completed steps toward your goal?

2. If you haven't completed any steps, how do you feel about falling short? What can you do about it?

3. When you need the help of others to achieve a goal, how can you build in that requirement as part of your plan?

You Can Reach Your Goals!
Experience Sheet

PART 1:

What are goals?

A goal is an end, home base, the final destination, what you are aiming for. Goals can center on having something —clothes, a car, money — or they can center on achieving — improving your grades, finishing school, going to college, having a career, becoming famous, gaining knowledge and honors.

Short-term and long-range goals:

Short-term goals include making phone calls, finishing your homework, cleaning your room, doing your chores, or making plans for the weekend. Long-range goals might include planning a trip for next summer, deciding to go to a trade school, a community college, or a university; saving money to buy something special; or making plans for your future career.

Take a look at your goals.

Take a few minutes to write down some of your goals. Check whether each goal is short-term or long-range, and write in the date by which you plan to accomplish it.

Goals are written in special ways.

They are:

- Positive (They contain no negative words.)
- Personal (They're about us, not others.)
- Written as though they are happening now or have already happened. (Never write them as though they are "going to" happen.)

GOAL #1

_____
_____
_____
_____

___ Short Term   ___ Long Range

Target Date _____

GOAL #2

_____
_____
_____
_____

___ Short Term   ___ Long Range

Target Date _____

GOAL #3

_____
_____
_____
_____

___ Short Term   ___ Long Range

Target Date _____

PART 2:

Goal Achievement Score Sheet

GOAL #1

Steps Toward Achieving My Goal:	Review Date	Step Achieved	Step Not Achieved
1. _____			
2. _____			
3. _____			
4. _____			

GOAL #2

Steps Toward Achieving My Goal:	Review Date	Step Achieved	Step Not Achieved
1. _____			
2. _____			
3. _____			
4. _____			

GOAL #3

Steps Toward Achieving My Goal:	Review Date	Step Achieved	Step Not Achieved
1. _____			
2. _____			
3. _____			
4. _____			

Tips for Setting Goals
Experience Sheet

1. <u>Goals must be clear and describe exactly what you want or will do.</u>

2. <u>Goals must be personal.</u> They must be about you, not someone else.

3. <u>Goals must be measurable.</u> You need to know when you have achieved your goal.

4. <u>Goals must have realistic time limits.</u>

5. <u>Goals must be manageable.</u> Divide big goals into several smaller, attainable goals or tasks. This will enable you to experience results in a shorter period to time.

6. <u>Goals must be stated in positive rather than negative terms:</u> (I *will* do something rather than I *won't* do something.)

7. <u>Goals must be written down.</u> People are more likely to achieve goals that are in writing. Written goals can be reviewed regularly, and have more power. Like a contract with yourself, they are harder to neglect or forget.

I Do My Best in School When...
A Sharing Circle

Objectives:
Group members will:
—describe the conditions under which they perform best in school.
—state how they can increase the incidence of those conditions.

Introduce the Topic:
Today's Sharing Circle topic is, "I Do My Best in School When...." School is not always the easiest place to be, and performing well in school can be a real challenge. We all do better in some situations than in others. And we all have certain conditions we prefer. What does it take for you to do your best in school?

Do you perform best when your teacher seems to respect you and expect a lot of you? Do you find it necessary to like a teacher in order to do well in a class? Maybe you do your best at school when things are going well at home or in your relationships with friends. Or perhaps you have found that it helps to set specific goals in your subjects. Do you do better in school when you've had extra sleep the night before, or when you've eaten a good breakfast? What effect does looking attractive and feeling good about yourself have on your school performance? Consider the circumstances under which you do your best in school, and tell us about one. The topic is, "I Do My Best in School When...."

Discussion Questions:
1. What seem to be our biggest motivators for doing well in school?
2. How can you create the conditions under which you do best more often?
3. What new insights have you gained from today's circle?

How I Learn Best
A Sharing Circle

Objectives:
Group members will:

—identify their preferred learning style.
—describe ideal learning conditions and recognize that not all school situations provide them.

Introduce the Topic:
In this Sharing Circle, we're going to talk about, "How I Learn Best." We all have certain things we do that help us learn. What are your most effective ways of learning? Do you like to work by yourself, or do you prefer to discuss the material you are studying with someone else? Do you learn best by reading information, or do you need to hear it or write it down? Some people learn best when they are involved in a project that allows them to get involved in some kind of physical activity, such as building something. We all have different methods of learning things. Take a few moments to think about your favorite methods. The topic is, "How I Learn Best."

Discussion Questions:
1. What causes us to differ in the ways we learn best?

2. How does awareness of your learning style help you?

3. What could this school do to make learning easier for you?

Things I Can Do to Get Where I Want to Be
A Sharing Circle

Objectives:
Group members will:

—identify a school-related goal.
—describe specific steps they can take now to reach their goal.

Introduce the Topic:
Today's topic is, "Things I Can Do to Get Where I Want to Be." The theme of this topic is very important to consider when you want to achieve something. To reach any kind of a goal, it is very important to think of all the steps you will have to take. This is true whether your goal is immediate, like getting a good grade on a test, or long term, like wanting to attend a major university in another city. Whatever it is, you need to be aware of all the things it takes to get what you want.

Think of one of your goals. Choose one that is related to, or will be affected by, your school performance. Now try to picture yourself doing everything necessary to reach that goal. Do you have to learn a new skill or language? Do you have to read books or talk with people in order to get information? Will you have to change your way of thinking, or strengthen your body, or get rid of a bad habit? This is a complex topic, so take your time. Tell us your goal, and then name all the things you can start doing now. When you're ready to share, the topic is, "Things I Can Do to Get Where I Want to Be."

Discussion Questions:
1. Why is it important to be aware of what it takes to reach a goal?

2. What similarities did you notice in the steps we need to take to reach our goals? What differences did you notice?

3. What can happen if you continually put off taking that first step toward your goal?

CHANGING FAMILY GROUPS

NOTE: The activities in this section involve potentially sensitive issues and therefore may not be suitable for all students. Please review each activity carefully prior to use, making whatever modifications are necessary for the age, maturity, and culture of your students, the policies of your school, and the conventions of your community.

Family Discovery Maps
Art Activity and Sharing

Procedure:
Begin by asking the students to take a few moments to think about the highlights of their family life. Suggest that they go back in their minds through the years and recall special events, fun times, and — in particular — significant changes.

Have the students take a sheet of paper and write at the top, "Family Discovery Map." (If you don't have art materials, the students can use their own notepaper and pens or pencils.)

Put the same heading on the board or a piece of chart paper. Then, draw a winding road or highway extending from the bottom of the sheet to the top. Ask the students to draw a similar road on their paper — straight or winding, two-lane or eight, but extending across the page. At one end of the road, tell them to write in the year of their birth; at the other end, the present year.

Next, tell the students to draw six signs along the road. They can look like freeway markers, billboards, speed limit signs, or any other type of signpost, as long as they are large enough to contain a few words. Demonstrate by drawing four signs on your road. Then explain:

These signs represent six significant events in your family life. So think of six things that really stand out as highlights or turning points in your journey together. They don't all have to be positive experiences. In fact, some may be negative. If they had an impact on you and

Objectives:
Group members will:

—identify significant events in their family life to date.
—envision and describe future events that they want their family to experience.

Materials:
drawing paper and colored markers (optional); board or chart paper

your family, if they changed the direction of your life together, they belong on the map. Put them in the order they occurred. Write a very brief description of each event on one of the signs.

When the students have finished, tell them to turn their paper over and draw another road on the opposite side. Have them label this road, "Family Future Map." In your words, explain:

Now your job is to chart a future for your family. What do you want the coming years to be like? Draw four signs and, on each sign, describe one event or change that you think is very important to your family's future. These are the goals *that you have for your family. Consider carefully. Envision and then draw exactly what you want.*

Invite the students to share their maps with the group. Have them hold up and explain their "Family Discovery Map" first, and then turn it over and explain the "Family Future Map." Facilitate discussion throughout the sharing period.

Discussion Questions:

1. What similarities and differences did you notice in the events we consider significant?

2. Did you discover any kind of pattern in your own map or someone else's? Explain.

3. What kinds of events can actually change the direction of a family?

4. What kinds of events can cause a family to go off the road temporarily?

5. What kinds of events make for a smooth, enjoyable ride?

6. How do you feel about the future you designed for your family?

7. How much control do you have over those future events?

8. What did you learn about your family life from this activity?

The Ups and Downs of Family Life
Experiment and Discussion

Procedure:
Begin by talking about the high and low points that we all experience in our lives. Point out that all life forms seem to go through cycles — and cycles within cycles. Clouds form from moisture, fall as rain, and form again. Plants flower, and wilt, and flower again. Animals and humans are born, grow, age, and die. While we live, people experience many smaller "births" (opportunities) and "deaths" (losses) and each one contributes to our unique identity.

Have the students take a sheet of paper. Across the top of the sheet, and parallel to each other, tell the students to describe three positive family events that happened recently or are going to happen soon. Across the bottom of the sheet, and parallel to each other, tell the students to describe two negative events.

Have the students connect the events with a single line that goes from the first event at the top to the first event at the bottom, to the second event at the top, to the second event at the bottom, and back to the third event at the top. The configuration of the line will be similar to a large **W**, with the positive experiences forming three peaks at the top, and the negative experiences forming two valleys at the bottom.

Objectives:
Group members will:

—identify specific positive and negative events in their family life.
—describe the positive aspects of negative events.
—explain how their own attitudes and beliefs affect positive and negative views.

Materials:
writing materials

Direct the students to sit with a partner and describe what they have written on their sheet. Urge them to talk about what each event means to them personally. As listeners, encourage the students to use active listening skills and reflect feelings.

When both partners have had an opportunity to share, direct them to turn their papers upside down, so that the negative events become peaks, and the positive events become valleys. In your own words, say to the students:

Now I want you to talk to your partner about the positive aspects of those negative events. Almost everything that happens to us offers some kind of benefit. Maybe the benefits have always been their, but you have never recognized them before. The death of a loved one can cause those who are left to grow closer to one another. A divorce can result in a more peaceful home environment, a new career for Mom, or greater self-sufficiency for you. A lost job can lead to new ways of doing things, greater respect for money, or regular help with homework.

Give the students time to share and discuss the "highs within their lows," and then reconvene the group for debriefing and closure.

Discussion Questions:

1. Were you unable to find positive elements in some of your lows? Which ones and why?

2. What determines whether a negative event has some kind of positive outcome? (our own attitudes, openness, willingness to change)

3. Is it possible to have a life without valleys? What would happen to the peaks in such a life? How would such a life look and feel?

4. What have you learned about your family life from this activity? What have you learned about yourself?

Communicating with Parents
Dyads and Discussion

Procedure:
Announce that today the group is going to be talking about ways of communicating with parents that produce good and not-so-good results. For example, you might say:

When changes take place in your family, whether through divorce, death, the addition of a child, or some other event, we need to be able to talk frequently with our parents. One thing we can do in this group is examine some of the problems we have communicating with our parents, and see if we can come up with better ways of going about it.

Ask the students to form dyads. Explain that you will be announcing a topic, and that one partner will speak to that topic for 2 minutes while the other listens actively. Then the other partner will have 2 minutes to speak to the same topic. Tell the students that there are five topics all together, and that you will be asking them to switch partners for each new topic.

Objectives:
Group members will:
—identify problems communicating with parents.
—describe how they can improve their own communication.
—identify the best time to talk to parents.

Materials:
board or chart paper

Write the first topic on the board and direct the pairs to begin. After 2 minutes, signal them to switch roles. After 2 more minutes, have the students change partners. Write the next topic on the board and repeat the process.

Topics:

When I'm Upset With My Parent, I...

When My Parent Gives Me Advice, I Feel...

I'm Afraid to Tell My Parent...

I Need to Talk to My Parent About...

The Best Time to Talk to My Parent Is...

After all five topics have been addressed, reconvene the group and facilitate debriefing and discussion.

Discussion Questions:

1. Why do we have difficulty communicating with parents?

2. What did you discover about the *way* you communicate with your parent?

3. What makes us afraid to talk to our parents about certain things?

4. How will problems get solved if we don't talk honestly to each other?

5. How can you improve your communication with your parents?

6. If you have a busy parent who never seems to have time to talk, would you be willing to make an appointment with him/her? What would be the best time of day and how would you go about it?

7. If you could change one thing about the way your parent communicates with you, what would it be?

Stuck in the Middle
Role Play and Discussion

Procedure:

Initiate a discussion about some of the problems that occur as families make adjustments associated with divorce, remarriage, death, and other changes. Talk about the feelings that different members of the family have and how those feelings sometimes produce conflict. Point out that conflicts like these can put kids right in the middle.

Distribute the "Role Play Situations." Explain that the students are going to act out these scenarios as a way of getting in touch with the feelings of different family members and practicing effective communication.

Depending on the size of your group, the students may need to act in more than one role play. For this reason, try to keep the dramatizations as extemporaneous as possible. Choose the cast, allow 1-2 minutes for preparation, and then launch right into the role play.

After each role play, facilitate debriefing and discussion.

Objectives:
Group members will:

—identify the feelings and motivations of family members in conflict situations.
—practice assertive communication.

Note: This activity works best if the students have received practice in the use of I-messages and/or assertiveness techniques. If they have not, you may wish to introduce I-messages as part of the activity.

Materials:
one copy of the Role Play Situations for each student; articles of clothing and props (optional)

Discussion Questions:

To the actors:

1. How did you feel in your role?

2. What insights did you gain about the needs/desires of the person you played?

3. What do you think the other characters in your scenario were thinking and feeling?

4. If you were in a real situation similar to this, what would you do?

To the observers:

1. What was the real problem in this situation?

2. Who was "right" and who was "wrong?"

3. Did the person who was "wrong" do this to be mean? What caused him/her to do it?

4. If you were the kid in this situation, how would you have handled it?

Role Play Situations

1. Your bike (computer, clarinet, etc.) needs repairs, so your mom drops it off to be fixed. Then she makes you telephone your dad and ask him to include extra money in his child support payment to cover the bill. He gets mad and yells at you.

Roles: mom, dad, you

2. You are going to be in a school play (piano recital, dance concert, etc.). You invite your dad, but your mother won't allow him to attend the cast party afterwards. You want him to be there.

Roles: mom, you

3. Since your mother left, your dad expects you to do all the things that she used to do — housework, cooking, laundry, and shopping. Your brother, who is a year older, doesn't have to do any of these things.

Roles: dad, you, brother

4. Your parents are divorced and you live with your mom. When your dad's mother dies, your mom won't let you attend the funeral. She says that your grandmother always hated her and broke up the marriage. But you loved your grandmother and she was always nice to you.

Roles: mom, you

5. You are spending the weekend with your dad, and on Saturday he takes you with him to visit his new girlfriend. Suddenly, your mother shows up. She's furious, and threatens to revoke your dad's visitation rights.

Roles: dad, girlfriend, mom, you

6. You are visiting your mom. When it's time to leave, your new stepmother picks you up instead of your dad. Your mom refuses to let you go and the two women almost get into a fight.

Roles: mom, stepmother, you

7. You and your new stepbrother are arguing over which TV show to watch. Your stepmother interrupts, tells you to stop being so selfish, and hands the remote control to your stepbrother. You think she always sides with him.

Roles: stepbrother, stepmother, you

8. After your grandfather dies, your mother has a big yard sale to dispose of his things. A neighbor says to you during the sale, "This is disgraceful. Don't your have any respect for that dear old man?"

Roles: neighbor, you

9. You find a really nice photo of your dad, which you frame and put beside your bed. When you get home from school the next day, it's gone. Your mom tells you that she won't have any pictures of "that creep" displayed in the house.

Roles: mom, you

10. When your mom remarries, she begins attending services at your new stepfather's church (synagog, temple, etc.). She tells you that you have to go, too. You want to continue attending the church where your father goes.

Roles: mom, stepfather, you

Problems, Problems!
Experience Sheet and Letter Writing

Procedure:

Introduce the activity by acknowledging that all people experience problems from time to time in their families. Sometimes the problems are small and sometimes they are complicated and serious. If appropriate, remind the students that the purpose of the group is to help members deal with changing circumstances at home.

Distribute the experience sheet. Explain that the sheet is designed to help them express their thoughts and feelings concerning a current family problem. Go over the directions, and then give the students a few minutes to complete the sheet.

When they have completed the experience sheet, ask the students to take out a blank sheet of paper and write a "Dear Abby" letter concerning the problem they just examined. Tell them to summarize their main concerns and state what kind of help they desire. Offer examples, as needed. Suggest that the students sign their letters with fictitious names, such as "Worried Most of the Time."

Objectives:

Group members will:

—examine aspects of a current family problem.
—anonymously describe their problem and seek advice.
—offer suggestions for solving the problems of others.

Materials:

one copy of the experience sheet, "Looking at a Problem," for each student; box with a slot for collecting "mail;" note paper for letter writing

Collect the letters in a box.

One at a time, remove the letters and read them aloud to the group, respecting the anonymity of the author. If the group is large, you may want to spread this over several sessions so that the exercise does not become too repetitious. Engage the group in a discussion of the situation, and invite group members to suggest ways of dealing with the problem.

Invite the students to write personal responses to the letters. Tell them to address their responses to the fictitious name used by the author and place them in the box at any time. Occasionally, check the box and make sure that the students receive all replies.

Discussion Questions:

1. What kinds of problems are typical in families?

2. Was it helpful to write about your problem? In what ways?

3. How can you make sure that you have regular opportunities to talk to you parent(s) about what is going on?

4. Who are some other people that you can turn to for help?

5. What would you like to say to other students who are having problems similar to yours?

Looking at a Problem Experience Sheet

Finish the sentences below. Try not to think about your answers too much. Just put down what you are really feeling. You don't have to show this paper to anyone if you don't want to. If you get stuck on a sentence, skip to the next one.

A problem that is going on in my family right now is _____

When I first learned about this problem, I felt _____

My role in the problem is _____

Things I don't understand about the problem are _____

What I would like to say to my mother is _____

What I would like to say to my father is _____

To solve this problem, I think we should _____

When I think about the future, I _____

How I feel about the problem now is _____

Dealing with Loss
Presentation, Sharing, and Discussion

Objectives:
Group members will:

—describe a personal loss.
—discuss the five stages of dealing with loss.
—identify the stage they are presently in and the feelings they are experiencing.

Materials:
board or chart paper

Procedure:
Begin this activity by introducing students to the topic of loss. For example you might say:

We experience many kinds of loss in our lives — the death of a family member or friend, the loss of a parent through divorce, friends moving away, a pet dying, a relationship breaking up. When something like this happens, our strong feelings can make it very difficult to cope. It helps to know that other people experience losses and get through them. It also helps to understand the stages our feelings go through as we adjust to the loss.

Ask the students to think of a loss they have experienced. Invite them to tell the group:

—*the nature of the loss (death, divorce, etc.)*
—*when it happened*
—*how they are feeling about it now*
—*any other details they would like to mention*

As the students share, model active listening, and facilitate discussion.

Next, introduce the five stages of loss first described by Elizabeth Kubler-Ross in her book *On Death and Dying*. As you explain each stage (suggested explanations appear in italics), invite the students to add observations from their own experiences. Taking the time to elicit their contributions will enrich the discussion immensely.

Stages of Loss

• Denial

When you know you are about to lose someone or something that you value, the first reaction is disbelief. "No, this can't be happening." "Everything will be okay tomorrow." "This is just a bad dream. I'll wake up soon."

• Anger

When you can no longer deny the loss, you experience frustration and anger. "What did I do to deserve this?" "How can s/he do that to me?" "This could only happen in an unfair, stupid world."

• Bargaining

After you express your anger, you may begin to feel hopeful again. You think, "Maybe if I'm a better person, Dad will stay." "If I promise to help take care of her, maybe God will let Grandma live." "I'll change all of my bad habits and then she'll like me again."

• Grieving

At this stage, you allow yourself to feel the pain and hurt. You may cry a lot and feel very depressed and hopeless. Difficult as it is, this is a very important stage. A person can't fully recover from a loss without grieving.

• Acceptance

Finally, you start to feel okay again. You may still be sad sometimes, but life returns to normal and you no longer think constantly about the person or condition you lost.

Point out that people don't always go through the stages in sequence. Sometimes they bounce back and forth between a couple of stages for a long time. In some cases, completing the cycle can take many months. Friends, relatives, and teachers who don't realize how long it can take may wonder why the person hasn't snapped out of it.

Use the remainder of the time to facilitate discussion concerning the stages.

Discussion Questions:

1. How many of the stages have you been through?

2. How did you feel at each stage and how did you behave?

3. Which of the five stages are you in right now?

4. Many people who want to help simply don't know what to do or say. What would you like them to do or say?

5. What have you learned from this activity?

A Letter to...
Guided Imagery, Writing, and Discussion

Objectives:
Group members will:

—recall a happy memory involving a person they have lost.
—express their feelings and thoughts by writing a letter to the person.

Materials:
writing paper; relaxing music (optional)

Procedure:
Have the students close their eyes and take a comfortable position. If you have music, begin to play it at a low volume. In a gentle but audible voice, read the following guided imagery exercise, pausing for at least 5 seconds between phrases.

Take a deep breath and let it out slowly.... Begin to relax your body and your mind.... Keep breathing deeply.... Feel the tension leave each part of your body.... Relax your feet and ankles ... your calves and thighs ... your hips, stomach, and chest ... your hands and arms ... your back, shoulders and neck ... your face.... And while you're relaxing, begin to think about the person you have lost. ... See the person exactly the way you like to remember him or her.... Picture everything in detail.... And with this image in your mind, begin to recall a happy memory that you shared with the person.... a vacation, a job that you did together, a meal.... Remember it in detail.... Recall the surroundings ... the sounds ... the aromas ... what you both were wearing ... what you said ... how you felt.... Keep breathing deeply while you relive completely that happy memory (pause 15 seconds).... Now, think of something that you would like to say to the person you lost.... If you could communicate with this person right now, what would your message be? ... Would you tell the person what you appreciated about him or her? ... Would you share the memory you just recalled? ... Would you ask a question? ... See yourself speaking to the person now (pause 15 seconds)

. . . When you are finished, say good-by to the person. . . . Take your time. . . . Know that you can revisit this person in your mind whenever you wish. . . . When you are ready, open your eyes and return to the group.

Give the students a few moments to readjust, quietly accepting any tears or other expressions of sadness.

Distribute the writing paper. Tell the students that you would like them to write down some of the thoughts and feelings they just experienced in the form of a letter to the person they lost. In your own words, explain:

You don't need to show this letter to anyone, so say whatever you want to say. Perhaps you'll want to write down the same words you said to the person in your imagination, or maybe you want to say something entirely different. It's up to you. Begin your letter with "Dear... " and the name with which you always addressed the person. Then, simply write. You'll have 15 minutes to complete your letter.

When the students have finished writing, you may wish to facilitate a culminating discussion.

Discussion Questions:

1. How has your life changed since you lost this person?

2. What is hardest about dealing with the loss right now?

3. What did you learn from the things we did here today?

A Favorite Family Memory
A Sharing Circle

Objectives:
Group members will:

—describe an enjoyable family event.
—discuss how memories help them deal with family changes.

Introduce the Topic:

Our topic today is, "A Favorite Family Memory." All of us have happy memories of times spent with our families — what's one of yours? Maybe what comes to mind is a holiday that you celebrated with a big family gathering and lots of wonderful food. Or maybe it's a vacation that you took together, or a special birthday party. On the other hand, perhaps you prefer to recall a more ordinary event, like working on a family project, or eating an evening meal, or playing a particularly lively board game.

Have you and your family ever gone together to pick out a new pet, find a holiday tree, or shop for a car? Do you remember a picnic, backyard barbecue, or shopping trip that was especially fun? Think about it for a few moments. If you decide to share, tell us what made the event so memorable, and the feelings you experienced at the time. The topic is, "A Favorite Family Memory."

Discussion Questions:

1. How do you feel when you talk about this family event today?

2. Why is it important to continue celebrating special moments through our memories?

3. When our families change, what other things besides memories help us adjust to new situations?

The Hardest Thing About Divorce
A Sharing Circle

Objectives:
Group members will:

—describe a difficult consequence of divorce.
—identify strategies for dealing with the negative results of divorce.

Introduce the Topic:
Our topic today is, "The Hardest Thing About Divorce." This is a topic that may take a little thought, because there aren't very many things about divorce that are pleasant. You may want to close your eyes and think quietly for a few moments. Of all the things that have happened as a result of the divorce in your family, which has been the worst? Maybe the hardest thing was seeing one of your parents physically move out of the house. Or maybe there was a lot of fighting in your home, and the tension was terrible. Perhaps you had to move to a new neighborhood and lost some of your friends in the process, or maybe your mom had to start working, so now you go home every day to an empty house. Divorce causes many changes, and few of them are easy to deal with. We probably all share many of the same feelings. The topic is, "The Hardest Thing About Divorce."

Discussion Questions:
1. What similarities did you hear in the things we shared?

2. Do some of the problems that were mentioned have solutions? Which ones, and what might those solutions look like?

3. Can you describe a positive result that can come from divorce?

4. Who can you talk to about your feelings? What other helpful things can you do?

When I'm a Parent, I Plan to...
A Sharing Circle

Objectives:
Group members will:

—describe attributes of an effective parent.
—express feelings associated with their own family relationships.

Introduce the Topic:
Our topic today is, "When I'm a Parent I Plan to..." Nobody knows for sure what the future will bring, but just for today let's assume that all of us will become parents. What is one quality that you intend to have as a parent, or one thing you intend to do? There are many ways you might finish this sentence, so see what comes to mind. Maybe you plan to listen well to your children, play with them every day, give them lots of hugs, read to them, or help them with their homework. Perhaps you plan to create a peaceful home life, make sure they get into sports, or always visit their teacher. Or maybe the thing you plan to do as a parent is limit the number of children you have. Think about it for a few minutes. Tell us what you would do and why. The topic is, "When I'm a Parent, I Plan to...."

Discussion Questions:
1. What made you decide that the thing you shared is so important?

2. How do we learn to be parents? Do you think people should be trained for parenthood? How?

3. What is one positive thing that *your* parent always does?

CULTURAL/RACIAL ISSUES

NOTE: The activities in this section involve potentially sensitive issues and therefore may not be suitable for all students. Please review each activity carefully prior to use, making whatever modifications are necessary for the age, maturity, and culture of your students, the policies of your school, and the conventions of your community.

Thumbprint Mural

Art Activity and Discussion

Objectives:
Group members will:
- describe differences among people.
- examine and compare their thumbprints.
- identify and appreciate some of their own differences.

Materials:
large sheet of butcher paper or newsprint, masking tape, colored markers, ink pad,

Procedure:
Tape the butcher paper or newsprint to a board or wall. Set out the ink pad and marking pens.

Announce to the group that the subject of this session is differences among people. Ask the students to think of all the ways in which they are different from one another. They will probably mention such things as hair, eye and skin color; facial features; names and birth dates; family differences; interests and abilities; etc.

If no one mentions fingerprints, point out that the uniqueness of fingerprints has made them a primary means of identifying one person from another.

Tell the students that they are going to have an opportunity to compare thumbprints. Press your own thumb to the ink pad and stamp your thumbprint on the butcher paper. Then, pick two or more colored markers and write your name and something unique about yourself in a circle, wavy line, or other pattern around the thumbprint. For example, you might write:

Ms. Patterson — makes the best spaghetti sauce in town.

One at a time, invite the students to add their thumbprints and statements to the mural. Ask them to read their statements aloud so that everyone can hear them.

Give the group an opportunity to closely examine the completed mural, noting the differences in thumbprints. Lead a culminating discussion.

Discussion Questions:

1. What makes our thumbprints different from one another?

2. How are our thumbprints alike?

3. Can you tell a person's religion or the color of his/her skin from a thumbprint? Why not?

4. Out of all the differences among people, why do you think such a big deal is made out of skin color?

5. What did you learn about someone in the group that you didn't know before?

6. What did you learn from this activity?

Facial Follies

Dyad Experiments and Discussion

Objectives:

Group members will:

—describe a partner's appearance in detail.
—state a conclusion about the person based on appearance.
—discuss the risks involved in making judgments based on appearance.

Materials:

board or chart paper

Procedure:

Write the following quotation on the board or chart paper so that the group members will see it when they enter the room:

Appearances often are deceiving.

—Aesop

Have the students choose partners. To the extent possible, create mixed racial pairings.

Ask the partners to sit facing each other, and to decide who is **A** and who is **B**. In your own words, give these directions:

Each of you will have 3 minutes to speak. The A's will go first, while the B's listen. Then the B's will talk while the A's listen. I will signal you when it is time to switch roles. When you are the speaker, you are to look at your partner and describe your partner from the neck up. Be as specific and descriptive as you can. For example, describe how the nose curves, the size and shape of the eyes, the thickness and position of the eyebrows, the way the mouth is shaped and the way it moves. If your partner's skin is brown, what shade of brown is it? Is it the shade of a pecan, a raisin, a polished oak table, or a copper kettle? What unique marks do you see on your partner's skin? How does your partner's hair grow? Does it remind you of cotton, mohair, straw, or rope? Really look at your partner. Notice every little thing you can, and see if you can put each detail into words.

Signal the pairs to begin. After 3 minutes signal them to switch roles. When the second speaker is finished, tell the partners to look directly at each other and take turns finishing this sentence:

Based on how you look, I believe that you are...

Have the students choose new partners and repeat the process. If time permits, repeat it a third time.

Debrief and discuss the experience.

Discussion Questions:

1. How did you feel when you were describing your partner?

2. How did you feel when you were being described?

3. What were some of the conclusions you arrived at based on the way your partner looked?

4. Did most of you choose safe, obvious conclusions or make risky judgments?

5. How did you react to the judgment made about you? Was it true, false, confusing, nonsensical?

6. What kinds of judgments do you make about people outside of this group based on their appearance?

7. What is your reaction to the quotation on the board?

8. What have you learned from this session?

Examining Stereotypes
Brainstorming and Discussion

Objectives:
Group members will:

—define the term stereotype.
—identify common stereotypes based on race.
—describe problems caused by stereotyping.
—suggest ways of reducing or eliminating harmful stereotypes at school.

Materials:
board or chart paper

Procedure:
Begin by asking the students to help you list different racial groups represented in the school. As each group is identified, write it as a heading on the board or a chart.

Next, define the word *stereotype*. Give the students plenty of time to debate/discuss various ideas. If they need help, here is one possible definition:

an oversimplified opinion or mental picture held in common by members of a group

When the students have a good grasp of the concept, engage them in brainstorming a list of stereotypes for each of the racial groups listed. In your own words, explain: *What oversimplified ideas and opinions do we have of each other based on race? What have you heard adults or kids say, seen on TV, or learned through jokes, music, or movies?*

Encourage the students to be candid by setting a matter-of-fact, non judgmental tone. Depending on the age, sophistication, and trust level of the group, you may generate items such as:

Whites
self-centered; anti-family
only care about money
violent; worship violent heros
racist

Latinos
poor
lazy; don't want to study or work
don't treat women equally
have too many children

Blacks
athletic
drug users and dealers
violent
less intelligent

Asians
smart; best students
meek; unassertive
unathletic
form cliques; exclude others

Next, ask the students: *Which stereotypes do you think exist widely at our school? Which ones are interfering with our ability to show everyone equal respect and include all students equally in activities?*

Go through the lists and check off those items that the students think are causing problems.

Have the students work in teams of three or four. Instruct them to take only those stereotypes that were checked and rank them from "most harmful" to "least harmful." Then have the teams discuss ways of reducing or eliminating the top two on their ordered lists.

Allow the teams to work for about 15 minutes. Then have them present their rankings to the rest of the group along with their ideas for eliminating or reducing the most serious stereotyping. Lead a culminating discussion.

Discussion Questions:

1. Why do groups stereotype each other?

2. How do stereotypes get started? How do they stay alive?

3. How can we keep from making assumptions about people we don't know?

4. What can you do personally to eliminate stereotyping here at school? ...at home?

Inside, Outside

Game and Discussion

Procedure:

In your own words, explain to the students:

I am going to place a colored dot on the forehead of each person. The color of your dot will determine what group you will join. However, you will not be able to see your own dot. In addition, there will be <u>no talking</u> during the activity. You will form your groups through nonverbal interaction — facial expressions, body language, gestures, etc.

Restate the rules of the game:

1. No talking

2. Use nonverbal behavior to discover the color of your dot.

3. Form a group with other students who are wearing the same color dot.

Signal the beginning of the "no talking" period. Go around and place a dot on the forehead of each student. (Do not allow the students to see their own dots.)

Objectives:

Group members will:

— simulate the experiences of being included and excluded.
— describe feelings associated with inclusion and exclusion.
— identify benefits that can result from including others.
— specify ways to include others in their activities.

Materials:

adhesive colored dots in at least three colors, including yellow

Depending on the number of students, use at least two colors to form groups of three or more. Place a yellow dot on the forehead of *only <u>one</u> student* — preferably one who is well liked and accepted.

Instruct the students to stand, begin moving around, and *silently* form their groups. The students will quickly realize that one person has been left out and is not a part of any group.

Call an end to the "no talking" period. Ask the student with the yellow dot to tell the group how s/he felt. Then lead a culminating discussion, focusing on issues of inclusion, exclusion, and discrimination.

Discussion Questions:

1. How does it feel to be included? ...excluded?

2. What are some of the bases upon which we exclude people?

3. When specific people are always excluded, what kinds of problems can result?

4. What are some benefits of including others?

5. What can you do to include more students in your activities?

How Would You Feel?
Experience Sheet and Discussion

Procedure:

Distribute the experience sheets. Give the students time to fill them out. If you want to encourage longer, more thoughtful responses, ask the students to complete them between sessions.

Note: Allow the students to approach the questions in any way they choose. Some of the questions are worded so that they may represent the view of either a minority or a majority person. This ambiguity could add interest to the discussion.

Ask the students which question they want to discuss first. Give students who are particularly troubled or confused by an item the opportunity to air their concerns. Encourage the sharing of personal experiences similar to those described.

If your group is large, have the students share in dyads before convening a group discussion. As each item is discussed, ask the questions listed below along with other relevant open-ended questions.

Objectives:
Group members will:

—examine racial/cultural issues.
—describe feelings related to racial issues.

Materials:
one copy of the experience sheet, "Put Yourself in This Situation" for each student

Discussion Questions:

1. What is really going on in this situation?
2. What would your very first feelings be in this situation? What about later?
3. What do you think you would say or do in this situation?
5. What if anything would you like to see done about this kind of situation? What are *you* willing to do?

Put Yourself in This Situation
Experience Sheet

Describe how you would feel in each of these situations:

How would you feel if...
- You had to pay "up front" before being served at a restaurant?

- The fences and walls in your once nice neighborhood were being covered with graffiti?

- You'd been waiting in a long line and when it was your turn, the clerk ignored you and went on to the next person?

- Women visibly clutched their handbags tighter when you passed them on the street?

- You couldn't get into the college you wanted because the rest of the openings were reserved for minorities?

- You were stopped for no apparent reason — other than your appearance — and asked to prove your legal residency?

- Your little brother/sister didn't understand the social slights and racial slurs of other kids, and you had to explain them to him/her?

- Your parents wouldn't let you date a person you really liked because of his/her race?

- People were always getting impatient — even angry — with you because of your heavy accent in English?

- You kept getting passed over for promotions, which went to workers less qualified than you?

- You were never invited when your friends went swimming at a private club?

- Your parent gently suggested that you spend less time with your friend of a different race?

Cultural/Racial Issues   Group Activities for Counselors

What Is Tolerance?
Current-Event Analysis and Discussion

Objectives:
Group members will:
—examine the issue of tolerance in the context of a current event.
—identify common acts of intolerance between individuals and groups.
—describe ways of demonstrating greater tolerance.

Materials:
a short news article about an incident relating to tolerance/intolerance between individuals or groups

Procedure:
Begin by reading the news article to the group. If the group is small, pass the article around and allow the students to examine it individually or in pairs. Then ask the group one or more of these questions:

—What is tolerance?
—What does it mean to be tolerant of another person or group?
—Who was tolerant/intolerant in this article?
—Toward whom was the tolerance/intolerance directed?
—What caused the tolerance/intolerance?
—What effects did the tolerance/intolerance have?

Ask the group to brainstorm ways in which different groups show intolerance toward each other. For example:

- different racial/ethnic groups
- boys and girls
- women and men
- different religions
- Democrats and Republicans
- straight people and gay people
- neighbors
- pet owners and non-owners
- adults who have children and childless adults
- thin people and fat people

Examples: Women shouldn't be fire fighters, run for President, or serve in combat units; people don't like to see men cry; an earring means a man is gay; boys are teased for playing with dolls; people of different races who marry are scorned; black people have a harder time finding jobs; etc.

Lead a culminating discussion focusing on specific things that they and others can do to increase tolerance.

Discussion Questions:

1. How can people of different races become more tolerant of each other? What about religions?

2. What can you do to help ease neighborhood intolerance of two big dogs that are friendly, but sometimes bark or mess on other people's lawns?

3. What can you do if some of your friends are saying intolerant things about another kid who is fat? ...dresses differently because of his/her religion or culture? ...has a disability?

4. What can you do to show your tolerance of people and groups that are different from you?

How I Deal with Intolerance and Prejudice
A Sharing Circle

Objectives:
Group members will:
—describe their reactions to acts of intolerance and prejudice.
—evaluate the effectiveness of different kinds of responses.

Introduce the Topic:
Our topic today is, "How I Deal with Intolerance and Prejudice." Perhaps you can think of several different ways in which you have reacted to these things. If so, just tell us about the way you respond most often. You can describe your reaction to intolerance and prejudice directed at you, or directed at someone else in your presence. Or you might decide to tell us about intolerance and prejudice that you've discovered within yourself, and how you deal with that.

Do you get angry and challenge the other person? Do you show your disapproval with an icy stare and a cold manner? Are you assertive in expressing your opposing views? Or do you tend to ignore the person and act as if nothing happened? If you like, tell us about a specific time you responded this way, and describe how you felt. Our topic is, "How I Deal with Intolerance and Prejudice."

Discussion Questions:
1. How well does your method of dealing with prejudice and intolerance work?

2. What happens as a result of your method? Are you satisfied with the results?

3. What would happen if all the people who usually ignore intolerance started opposing it assertively?

I Have a Friend Who Is Different From Me
A Sharing Circle

Objectives:
Group members will:

—identify specific differences between themselves and their friends.
—demonstrate respect for differences in race, culture, lifestyle, and ability.

Introduce the Topic:
Today we are going to talk about friends who are different from us and what we like about them. The topic for this session is, "I Have a Friend Who Is Different From Me."

We are all alike in many ways, but we are also different. Today, I want you to think about a friend who is different from you in at least one major way — and tell us why you like this person so much. Perhaps your friend is of a different race, or has a much larger family, or is many years older than you. Does your friend speak a different language or eat a different way than you do? Does your friend have a disability that causes his or her lifestyle to be different from yours? Maybe your friend celebrates birthdays differently than you do, or has different holidays. Tell us what you enjoy about this person. Does your friend listen to you and share things with you? Does he or she invite you to go places? Do you have something in common like a love of sports, music, or computers? Think about it for a few minutes. The topic is, "I Have a Friend Who Is Different From Me."

Discussion Questions:
1. What are some of the ways we differ from our friends?

2. How are you enriched by the differences between you and your friend?

3. What causes people to dislike other people because of things like race or religion?

4. What would our lives be like if we could only make friends with people who are just like we are?

I Judged a Person Based on Looks Alone
A Sharing Circle

Objectives:
Group members will:

—describe one way in which prejudiced opinions develop.
—define the term stereotyping and relate it to a personal experience.
—explain why judgments based on outward appearances are unreliable.

Introduce the Topic:
Today our topic is, "I Judged a Person Based on Looks Alone." It may not be fair, but this is something we all do from time to time. See if you can think of an example from your own experience that you'd be willing to share. Maybe you felt disgusted when you saw a fat woman, or were uneasy when you passed a raggedly dressed man on the street. Perhaps you assumed that someone couldn't speak English, just from the color of his skin. Or maybe you had someone pegged as a rich snob just because she drove a fancy car. Have you ever had a negative impression upon seeing someone and later discovered that he was really nice? Have you been attracted to someone, and later found out that she was self-centered or boring? Think back and see if you can recall an instance like this. Tell us what you concluded about the person and why. And if you changed your opinion later, explain what influenced you. The topic is, "I Judged a Person Based on Looks Alone."

Discussion Questions:
1. What is meant by the term *stereotyping*? Was what you did a form of stereotyping? Was it a form of prejudice? Explain.

2. What causes people to have prejudiced reactions to others?

3. What's dangerous about judging "a book by its cover?"

4. How can you keep yourself from formulating snap judgments?

SOCIAL/SEXUAL HARASSMENT

NOTE: The activities in this section involve potentially sensitive issues and therefore may not be suitable for all students. Please review each activity carefully prior to use, making whatever modifications are necessary for the age, maturity, and culture of your students, the policies of your school, and the conventions of your community.

What If...?
Speculation and Discussion

Objectives:
Group members will:

—project themselves into hypothetical situations involving social/sexual harassment.
—describe their feelings and behaviors in these situations.
—identify effective ways of preventing/combating harassment.

Materials:
paper and pencils for note taking

Procedure:
If your group is fairly large, ask the students to form teams of three or four and give each team one "What if..." situation to discuss. If the group is small, include everyone in a single discussion. Select appropriate questions from the "Discussion Questions," below, to stimulate thinking and interaction.

If the students work in smaller groups, ask them to take notes. Have each group report its thoughts and conclusions to the total group.

What if...

- The other boys tease you because you enjoy cooking and baking.

- You are the only girl in a computer-project team and your teammates ignore your suggestions because you're "just a girl."

- You are being pressured by your friends to smoke cigarettes, even though you don't like the taste or smell.

- A close friend of your parents pays a visit when you are home alone and touches you in a way that makes you uncomfortable.

- Your older sister tells you that her boyfriend wants her to have a baby "to prove that she loves him."

- Several of your friends have formed a cheating ring at school — trading answers, making crib notes — and are after you to participate.

- You can't join a club or team because of your sex.

- A cruel rumor has been going around about a particular student. Now it has become "cool" to talk about this person, so almost everyone is doing it.

- Some boys have started talking about girls in sexual terms, making sure that the girls hear some of their comments.

- A friend threatens to stop talking to you if you don't back up a lie that she has told to her parents.

- You find out that you are the subject of sexually explicit graffiti in the boys/girls restroom.

Discussion Questions:

1. How do you think you would feel if you were involved in a situation like this?

2. How would you act? What would you do?

3. Where do we get our ideas about the roles of males and females?

4. What is sexual harassment?

5. How can you let a person know that you don't like his/her behavior and you want it to stop?

6. What is the difference between a caring touch and a touch that is inappropriate or makes you feel uncomfortable?

7. Who are some trusted adults that you can go to for help?

8. Is it possible to prevent people from harassing you? How?

Sexual Stereotypes
Brainstorming and Discussion

Objectives:
Group members will:
—define the term stereotype.
—identify common stereotypes based on gender.
—describe the effects of trying to conform to stereotypes.

Materials:
board or chart paper; one copy of the experience sheet, "The Cost of Conforming" for each student

Procedure:
Begin by asking the students to define the word *stereotype*. Give them plenty of time to debate/discuss various ideas. If they need help, here is one possible definition:

an oversimplified opinion or mental picture held in common by members of a group

When the students have a good grasp of the concept, engage them in brainstorming a list of stereotypes for males and females. In your own words, explain: *What oversimplified ideas and opinions do we have of each other based on gender? What stereotyped images of females and males do get from TV, music, videos, movies, advertising, other kids, and adults?*

Encourage the students to be candid by setting a matter-of-fact, non judgmental tone. Depending on the age, sophistication, and trust level of the group, you may generate items such as:

Males
- strong
- rugged
- take charge
- seldom cry or show feelings
- obsessed with sex
- athletic
- dominant/in control
- good at solving mechanical/technological problems

Females
- pretty/cute/beautiful
- emotional
- sexy
- thin
- flirtatious
- soft
- submissive/passive
- poor in math and technology

Next, ask the students: *Which of these stereotypes do you think exist widely at our school? Which ones define what kids at this school think of as the "ideal boy" and "ideal girl."*

Go through the lists and check off those items that the students think contribute to sexual stereotyping at the school.

Distribute the experience sheets. Go over the questions to ensure that the students understand them. Give the students a few minutes to complete their sheets. Then have them share what they have written with a partner. Lead a follow-up discussion.

Discussion Questions:

1. How much effort are you putting into trying to fit the stereotype for your gender?

2. What would happen if you quit trying to be like the ideal boy or girl?

3. Which price is higher, the price of trying to be something you're not, or the price of not conforming to the "ideal."

4. Why do we stereotype ourselves and each other?

5. How do stereotypes get started? How do they stay alive?

6. How does sexual stereotyping contribute to sexual discrimination? harassment?

The Cost of Conforming
Experience Sheet

What is your image of the ideal person of your age and sex? Describe him/her here:

_____
_____
_____
_____
_____
_____
_____

What price are you paying to fit that image?

_____
_____
_____
_____
_____
_____
_____

What are you doing to try to fit that image?

_____
_____
_____
_____
_____
_____
_____

What would happen if you dared to be different from that image?

_____
_____
_____
_____
_____
_____
_____

Defining Sexual Harassment
Brainstorming, Sharing, and Discussion

Procedure:
Ask the students to help you define the term *sexual harassment*. Write their contributions on the board or chart. When the students are satisfied with their definition, ask them to compare it to the definition below, issued by the Equal Employment Opportunities Commission (EEOC). Explain that the EEOC is an agency of the United States Government.

Any unwelcome sexual advances, requests for sexual favors, and other verbal or physical conduct of a sexual nature.

Note: The object of the above exercise is not to have the students guess the "right" answer, but for them to do some thinking on their own before seeing an official definition.

If clarification is needed, paraphrase the definition in simpler language — particularly for younger students. Then ask the students:

— *What are sexual "advances?"*
— *What is meant by "requests for sexual favors?"*

Objectives:
Group members will:

—define sexual harassment.
—distinguish sexual harassment from sexual discrimination.
—share and discuss examples of sexual harassment.

Materials:
board or chart paper

— *What are some examples of "other verbal or physical conduct of a sexual nature?"*
— *What is the most important word in this definition? (unwelcome)*

Facilitate discussion, focusing on behaviors that are fairly typical of interaction between young people within the age range of your students. Point out that sexual harassment is a form of sexual discrimination. Elicit examples of sexual discrimination, such as:

- A girl is refused admission to a military prep school because of gender.
- Females are paid less than males for the same or comparable work.
- A teacher consistently calls on boys significantly more than girls during class.

Ask the students to share examples of sexual discrimination and/or harassment that they have experienced. Talk about what happened in each situation and the feelings that the incident caused.

Before closing the session, ask the students to bring a current events article concerning sexual harassment or sexual discrimination to the next session.

Discussion Questions:

1. Do you think most sexual harassment is intentional? Why or why not?
2. How are harassing behaviors learned?
3. What is gained by sexually harassing another?
4. If you have ever been sexually harassed, how did you respond?
5. Why is it important for young people to become aware of sexual discrimination in all its forms?

Developing Awareness of Sexual Discrimination
News Articles and Discussion

Objectives:
Group members will:

—identify factors that make sexual harassment illegal in the workplace.
—examine actual or alleged incidents of sexual discrimination.

Note: This activity is a follow-up to the activity, "Defining Sexual Harassment."

Materials:
current events articles related to sexual harassment and/or sexual discrimination (brought by you and the students, or found on the internet)

Procedure:
Remind the students of the definition of sexual harassment. Then point out that the government of the United States has made sexual harassment illegal in the workplace, when:

- a person could lose his/her job by refusing to submit.

- other work-related decisions (advancement, pay increases, assignments) are based on whether or not a person submits.

- the person cannot fulfill his/her job requirements effectively because of the harassment.

Ask the students to paraphrase their current events articles for the group. Discuss each one. If the article involves illegal workplace harassment, ask the students which of the three conditions (above) makes the behavior illegal. If the article is about any form of sexual harassment, ask them if the behavior involves:

- an unwelcome sexual advance.

- an unwelcome request for sexual favors.

- other verbal or physical conduct of a sexual nature.

Discussion Questions:

1. How would you feel if you were one of the people in this article? What would you do?

2. Does it matter whether or not the sexual discrimination was conscious and intentional? What does matter?

3. Did the people in this article view each other as equals? Explain.

4. Do you think that adults who respect each other as equals engage in harassing behaviors? Why or why not? What about young people?

Flirting and Harassment: What's the Difference?

Brainstorming and Discussion

Procedure:

Begin by asking the students:

— *Do you think that most students at this school like to flirt?*
— *How many of you occasionally enjoy flirting?*

Then ask:

— *Do you think that many students at this school have been sexually harassed?*
— *How many of you have either been sexually harassed or have sexually harassed someone else?*

In responding to your questions, the students will probably begin to appreciate the fine line that exists between sexual harassment and flirting. Tell them that the group is going to further examine the similarities and differences between these two categories of behavior.

Divide the students into two groups and provide both groups with chart paper and a marking pen. Have one group brainstorm examples of sexual harassment and the other brainstorm examples of flirting.

Objectives:

Group members will:

— distinguish between flirting and sexual harassment and describe the feelings each produces.
— discuss the importance of intention and interpretation in determining the differences between flirting and harassment.

Materials:

chart paper and marking pens; masking tape

Tell them that their examples can involve behaviors between students at school or away from school, between students and adults, or between adults in the workplace or elsewhere.

Next, have the sexual harassment group list, on a second sheet of chart paper, how it <u>feels</u> to be sexually harassed. Tell them to include all the feelings they can think of. Have the flirting group do the same with their topic.

Have the groups tape their lists to a wall for viewing and comparison. Focus on the similarities and differences between the two lists. Where the same basic behavior (e.g., winking, long looks, comments) appear on both lists, ask the students:

—*How can the same behavior produce such different feelings?*
—*What determines whether this behavior is flirting or sexual harassment?*

Write the words *intention* and *interpretation* on the board. Talk about the fact that intentions can be misinterpreted — for example, when a boy's *intention* is to flirt harmlessly but his actions cause the girl to feel threatened or embarrassed, what has actually occurred is a form of harassment. Usually intentions can be read fairly accurately by the way the smile, touch, gesture, or comment is delivered. A friendly, appreciative smile doesn't look the same as a leer. A lewd, suggestive gesture is rarely seen for anything but what it is.

Through discussion, help the students recognize that when a message is delivered, the final determination as to how that message is interpreted always rests with the receiver. It is the receiver who decodes the message. It is the receiver who determines the impact of the message.

Discussion Questions:

1. How do young people usually respond when someone flirts with them?

2. How do they respond when someone sexually harasses them?

3. If a girl dresses "sexy," does that mean she's inviting the advances of boys? Why or why not?

4. Do girls sexually harass boys? Why and how?

5. If you think your behaviors have been misinterpreted, what can you do?

6. What effect does peer pressure have on the behavior of a group of boys/girls toward members of the opposite sex?

7. What role does respect play in all of this? Would you harass a person you respect? Explain your reasoning.

Asserting Personal Rights
Experience Sheet and Discussion

Objectives:
Group members will:

—explain that all people have basic human rights.
—describe how asserting personal rights combats harassment.
—discuss situations in which they would like to assert their rights.

Materials:
one copy of the experience sheet, "My Personal Rights," for each student

Procedure:
Distribute the experience sheets. Read and discuss the rights, one at a time.

Give a personal example of a time you chose to assert your personal rights. Ask the students to refer to their experience sheet and identify the personal right(s) you were asserting in the situation. Then encourage the students to generate examples of similar situations in their own life, and ask the class to identify the right(s) being asserted in each case.

Give the students a few minutes to complete the second part of the experience sheet. Then, as a group, discuss their answers.

Ask the students to think of current situations in which they would like to assert their rights, but are having difficulty doing so. Ask them why they think it is hard to stand up for their rights. Record their ideas on the board. Reasons might include:

- Friends might resent your telling them things they don't want to hear.

- Standing up for your rights in a public place draws attention to you.

- Standing up to sexual harassment might make members of the opposite sex dislike you.

- A little voice tells you that you "asked for" or deserve the treatment you got.

- If you ask for something, you might be told, "no."

- Standing up for your rights can be frightening.

- Standing up for your rights takes energy, and you may not get what you want anyway.

- Some individuals don't think that young people have the same rights as adults and probably won't listen.

- Some people think that members of your sex don't have the same rights, and they won't listen.

My Personal Rights
Experience Sheet

I have:

1. The right to act in ways that promote my dignity and self-respect as long as the rights of others are not violated in the process.

2. The right to be treated with respect.

3. The right to say "no" and not feel guilty.

4. The right to experience and express my feelings.

5. The right to take time to slow down and think.

6. The right to change my mind.

7. The right to ask for what I want.

8. The right to refuse help and assistance.

9. The right to ask for information.

10. The right to make mistakes.

11. The right to feel good about myself.

12. The right to do less than I am humanly capable of doing.

Which "Right" is being exercised in each of the following situations. Put a number (1-12) next to each item:

___ Telling your teacher that you need clearer directions on an assignment.

___ Telling your boyfriend/girlfriend that you are annoyed by his/her constant company

___ Asking your parent for more allowance.

___ Asking someone to go out with you.

___ Saying you'd rather not participate in an activity with your friends.

___ Telling someone who is pressuring you that you aren't ready to make a decision.

___ Objecting to someone's labelling or stereotyping you by disability, race, or gender.

___ Not staying up till 2:00 a.m. in order to get an "A" on a test.

___ Saying that you don't want to go to the game after all.

___ Reporting an incident in which you were sexually harassed.

___ Refusing to make a decision until more facts are available.

___ Acknowledging that you screwed up without feeling guilty.

___ Enthusiastically describing an accomplishment to someone.

Mastering Assertive Communication
Experience Sheet and Role Play

Procedure:

Begin by talking with the students about the fact that they have a choice whether they communicate passively, aggressively, or assertively. Point out that sometimes people act passively or aggressively because they haven't learned *how* to be assertive. When this is the case, it is difficult for people to get their needs met or their ideas expressed. Ask the students:

— *Have you ever been harassed sexually or in any other way?*
— *How did you respond? (Most students report that they respond to sexual harassment by ignoring it.)*
— *Do you think incidents like this would happen less if you were more assertive?*

Distribute the experience sheets. Read the definitions of Aggressive, Passive, and Assertive together. Discuss the differences. Give some examples from your own experience. Have the students pair up, and test their ability to discriminate between the three types of responses by completing the remainder of the experience sheet. Instruct them to identify the personal rights that are being threatened or violated by the aggressive and passive responses in each example—and to specify whose rights those are.

Objectives:

The students will:

—describe the differences between assertive, aggressive, and passive behaviors.
—practice assertive and non assertive behaviors in role play situations.
—explain how assertive, aggressive, and passive behaviors affect situations involving harassment.

Materials:

one copy of the experience sheet, "Acting Assertively," for each student

Go over the answers in the larger group. Invite some of the dyad pairs to role play the different situations. Have them role play all three responses, and then discuss the differences between the three. Facilitate discussion throughout the role plays.

Discussion Questions:

1. How did you feel when you were being aggressive? ...passive? ...assertive?

2. How did you feel when you were on the receiving end of an aggressive response? ...a passive response? ...an assertive response?

3. How do you react when someone almost always responds aggressively, but disguises his or her responses with humor?

4. What causes people to respond passively?

5. Which kind of behavior is being demonstrated by harassment of any kind?

6. When you ignore incidents of sexual harassment, what kind of message are you giving the harasser?

7. What skills do you need to practice in order to become comfortably assertive?

Acting Assertively
Experience Sheet

What does it mean to be aggressive, passive, or assertive?

People are aggressive when they:

- intentionally attack, take advantage of, humiliate, hurt, harass, or put down others.
- act on the belief that others are not as important as they are.

People are passive when they:

- invite, encourage, or permit others to take advantage of or harass them.
- discount themselves and act as if others are more important than they are.

People are assertive when they:

- express themselves openly and honestly to communicate their needs, wants, or feelings, without demanding or discounting the wants, needs, or feelings of others.
- act according to the belief that all people including themselves are equally important and deserving of respect.

Decide which of the following responses are passive, aggressive, and assertive. What personal rights are being violated by each aggressive response? What personal rights are being violated by each passive response?

Sylvia starts flirting with Brad during the lunch break. At first he's flattered, but when she starts hanging on him he backs off. But Sylvia won't leave him alone. Finally, Brad responds:

1. "Sylvia, I feel really crowded when you come on to me that way. I'm not interested, so please don't do it anymore."

2. "Uh, err, ghees Sylvia. What's gotten into you?"

3. By pushing Sylvia away and yelling, "Get out of here, ugly, I don't want you!"

Natalie drives into the parking lot of a small mall, but all the handicapped spaces are taken, so she has to park in a regular spot and then struggle to remove her chair from the back seat. As she's passing one of the handicapped spaces, Barbara almost collides with a young man running to his car. She says:

1. "Thanks to you, Mister, I just had to struggle for 20 minutes getting out of my car. Maybe when you pay a fine, you'll stop being so selfish."

2. "Hi. I guess maybe you didn't notice that's a handicapped spot?"

3. "You violate my rights when you take a spot that's reserved for people with disabilities. I hope you won't do it again."

Julian offers to fix the chain on Raquel's bike. When she thanks him he replies, "If you really want to thank me, come here and give me a kiss." Raquel responds:

1. "I'd rather kiss a hyena than a jerk like you. Get out of my face!"

2. "I feel tricked when you offer to help me an then expect something in return. If 'thank you' isn't enough, please don't offer to help me again."

3. By making a face and riding off on her bike.

Andy returns a pair of jeans to the store because the zipper is broken. The clerk says:

1. "Yes, that's a broken zipper all right. Can I get you another pair?"

2. "Oh, I'm so sorry. I should have checked the jeans before I sold them to you. It's all my fault."

3. "You broke this zipper didn't you? Well, you're not going to cheat us!"

Marcia is walking down the hall when Hal comes up beside her, puts his arm around her waist, and whispers in her ear, "You look really good today, Marcia." Marcia stops and says:

1. "Excuse me, Hal. I hear my mother calling."

2. "Hal, I am a person, not a pretzel. I'd appreciate if you would keep your hands off me and treat me with a little respect."

3. "Get your filthy hands off me, you pervert, or you won't have any teeth left in your mouth!"

Lydia insists that Alice help her carry some things to the auditorium. Alice responds:

1. "I'm afraid I'll be late for English, but if you want me to, okay."

2. "What's the matter with you? Are your arms broken?"

3. I can't help you right now, Lydia. I have to get to my English class."

Trish has to pass a group of boys on her way class. As she walks by, they start a chorus of sounds and gestures that cause Trish to see red. She responds:

1. By looking straight ahead and hurrying past.

2. By making a gesture of her own and then walking over and slapping one of the boys across the face.

3. "I have a right to use this walkway without getting any grief from you. If you ever do that to me again, I'll report you."

Social/Sexual Harassment

One Advantage of Being Male/Female Is...
A Sharing Circle

Objectives:
Group members will:

—distinguish between stereotypes and legitimate limitations based on gender.
—describe how they are affected by stereotyping.

Introduce the Topic:
The topic of this Sharing Circle is, "One Advantage of Being Male/Female Is..." You get to complete the sentence. The word <u>advantage</u> implies the ability to do, be, or have something that members of the opposite sex <u>can't</u> (or probably wouldn't) do, be, or have. Take a moment or two to think about it. What can females do that males can't (or probably wouldn't) do, and what can males do that females can't (or probably wouldn't) do? What about wearing certain types of clothing, behaving in particular ways, or selecting jobs and careers? Think about how much freedom you have to do things, go places, and make other kinds of choices. Think about safety, too. Being safe and secure affects how free you are to choose. Pick an advantage that you value and tell us about it. The topic is, "An Advantage of Being Male/Female Is...

Discussion Questions:
1. Which of the things we mentioned are things that the opposite sex really *can't* do, and which are things they just *don't* do?

2. How do we learn that certain choices are not acceptable for males or for females?

3. Have you ever done something that wasn't considered "feminine" or "masculine?" How did you feel and how did others react?

4. How limiting is our list of "don'ts" for females? How limiting is the list for males?

I Was Labeled Based on Something I Couldn't Change
A Sharing Circle

Objectives:
Group members will:

—describe a time when they were stereotyped by labeling language.
—describe how they felt in response to being labeled.
—identify methods they can use to discourage the practice of labeling.

Introduce the Topic:
One of the problems with labels—even flattering labels—is that they limit people. They cause us to see the labeled person as whatever the label says, rather than as a complex, unique individual. Today, we're going to talk about our own experiences with being labeled, and how those labels caused us to feel and react. Our topic is, "I Was Labeled Based on Something I Couldn't Change."

Think of a time when someone, or a group of people, labeled you. Maybe the label had to do with your appearance, your athletic ability—or lack of it—or your way of walking. Perhaps you were labeled based on your sex, or your racial, ethnic, or religious background. People get stuck with labels based on hair color, height, weight, facial features—even the size of certain body parts. We label both females and males for being particularly attractive, and we have lots of labels for people with disabilities. Think of a label that you're dealing with now or one that you carried in the past. Tell us how you feel about that label and the effect it has had on your life. Think about it for a few moments. The topic is, "I Was Labeled Based on Something I Couldn't Change."

Discussion Questions:
1. How did most of us react to being labeled? What did we do about it?

2. Why do we label people? What purpose does it serve?

3. What can you do to discourage your peers from labeling one another?

4. What can you do to influence adults who thoughtlessly or maliciously use labels?

A Time I Stereotyped Someone
A Sharing Circle

Objectives:
Group members will:
—recall instances in which they stereotyped others.
—explain what stereotyping is and why people do it.
—identify ways of avoiding the tendency to stereotype.

Introduce the Topic:
Our topic today is, "A Time I Stereotyped Someone." People stereotype other people in many different ways. Anytime we decide that a person belongs to a certain "group" and then make judgments about the person based solely on what we think about the group, we are stereotyping. Tell us about a time when you did something like that. Have you ever made assumptions about another student based on the kids he or she seemed to hang out with? Maybe you've stereotyped someone based on clothes, hair style, body build, or skin color. Or perhaps you've stereotyped a person based on gender. Have you ever failed to listen to a girl's opinion because she was "just a girl?" Have you ever decided that a guy was "macho" because of his looks? Have you ever assumed that a person with a disability was retarded and then found out that he or she was as smart as you? Think about it for a few moments. Our topic is, "A Time I Stereotyped Someone."

Discussion Questions:
1. Why do we stereotype others? What do we get out of it?
2. How do you feel when you find out that your assumptions about a person were wrong?
3. What can you do to avoid stereotyping?